SPORTS FAN VIOLENCE
IN NORTH AMERICA

WITHDRAWN

SPORTS FAN VIOLENCE IN NORTH AMERICA

Jerry M. Lewis

Rowman & Littlefield Publishers, Inc.
Lanham • Boulder • New York • Toronto • Plymouth, UK

ROWMAN & LITTLEFIELD PUBLISHERS, INC.

Published in the United States of America
by Rowman & Littlefield Publishers, Inc.
A wholly owned subsidiary of The Rowman & Littlefield Publishing Group, Inc.
4501 Forbes Boulevard, Suite 200, Lanham, Maryland 20706
www.rowmanlittlefield.com

Estover Road
Plymouth PL6 7PY
United Kingdom

British Library Cataloguing in Publication Information Available

Library of Congress Cataloging-in-Publication Data
Lewis, Jerry M. (Jerry Middleton), 1937–
  Sports fan violence in North America / Jerry M. Lewis.
    p. cm.
  Includes index.
  ISBN-13: 978-0-7425-3979-2 (cloth : alk. paper)
  ISBN-10: 0-7425-3979-2 (cloth : alk. paper)
  ISBN-13: 978-0-7425-3980-8 (pbk. : alk. paper)
  ISBN-10: 0-7425-3980-6 (pbk. : alk. paper)
  1. Violence in sports—North America. 2. Sports spectators—North America.
I. Title.

GV706.7.L49 2007
306.4'83097—dc22   2007005415

Printed in the United States of America

⊗™ The paper used in this publication meets the minimum requirements of
American National Standard for Information Sciences—Permanence of Paper
for Printed Library Materials, ANSI/NISO Z39.48-1992.

Contents

1

Introduction to Sports Fan Violence in North America

In a large city after a championship football game, fans gathered in a central location to celebrate the victory of their favorite team. This celebration resulted in vandalism, teargassing by police, turned-over and burned automobiles, and arrested sports fans. This event could have happened in Manchester, England, or Lima, Peru, but it actually took place in Columbus, Ohio, in November 2002 after the Ohio State–Michigan football game (see chapter 6). Sporting events excite emotions. Often, the aftermath of such events is some degree of collective outburst on the part of jubilant or disappointed fans. Sporting events in the United States can lead to violent outbursts by groups of spectators, resulting in serious injuries or even death. Wann et al. (2001) point to the importance of studying sports riots as they devote a full section to the topic in their book on sports spectators. Particularly useful is their chapter 7 on the types of fan violence.

This book is written in the collective behavior tradition, which is uniquely an American subspecialty of sociology. The study of collective behavior was born in the work of Robert Park at the University of Chicago and extended by the scholarship of Herbert Blumer, also of the University of Chicago. Collective behavior scholars study a range of topics, including rumors, disasters, and panic behavior, but the primary focus has always been on crowds. In studying crowds, the collective behavior tradition looks at rare events that have continuing impacts on society. To mention a few, one might note the Zoot Suit Riots in 1943, the Martin Luther King assassination riots in 1968, the Democratic Convention crowds in 1968, the Stonewall riots of 1969, the Kent State student protests in 1970, and the Los Angeles (Rodney King) riots in 1992. Earlier in American history there were the Boston Massacre in 1770, the New York City draft riots in 1863, and the Haymarket Square riot in 1886.

In this book, I discuss riots that occur in association with organized sport, particularly those that I have chosen to call celebrating riots—those violent events carried out by the fans of a winning sports team. In contrast, punishing riots are acts of collective violence carried out by the fans of the losing team. Celebrating riots are more typical of the North American sport cultures than are punishing riots. It should be noted that the term *riot* is one that is generally not used by collective behavior scholars who prefer the more neutral concept of temporary gatherings. However, I have retained the use of the word *riot* as it is part of the general public's discussions of these events.

When a sports riot happens it affects many constituencies (U.S. Department of Education 2003, 4), including peers, often fellow students, of the rioters; town-gown relations, in the case of collegiate sports riots; the local EMS (emergency medical service) personnel—police, fire, and ambulance services; businesses; local governments short of funds; and residents who share the tax burden. When it occurs in a university context, fan violence also has negative consequences for alumni, who do not like to hear and read the negative publicity that a sports riot brings to their university or community in which they typically take great pride.

While I hope this book is useful for the work of professional sociologists, it is directed to these various constituencies. For students, the analyses will help them understand why their fellow students act in the manner that they do in the context of the sporting event. For EMS personnel, the ideas presented here may help them prepare for and prevent future fan violence.

Businesses need to prepare for the celebrations that take place after major sports victories, and this book may help in guiding these preparations. In regard to local governments, while this book will not ease the tax burden, it may help mayors and other city officials to be more effective and efficient in planning and executing responses to potential or actual sports fan violence. Residents of a community where fan violence takes place may find understanding of that violence and the social-control responses to it. For alumni, understanding of the violence by students and others may help ease the embarrassment such riots bring to them.

Each chapter in the book is designed to stand alone. However, all of them together provide the reader with a detailed understanding of sports fan violence. Chapter 2 discusses theoretical approaches to fan violence drawn from the collective behavior tradition. From the structural-functional perspective is Neil J. Smelser's value-added model. The symbolic-interaction perspective is represented with the category system of Clark McPhail. Smelser's structural-functional theory allows the analyst to look at the general conditions that lead to sports fan violence. I argue that this theory is particularly useful in the management of the large amounts of data that are often generated by those sports riots that gain considerable media attention. McPhail's categories facilitate the analyst's ability to actually write about the behavior of the actors carrying out the fan violence. A theory of celebrating riots is presented in chapter 6.

Chapter 3 presents an approach to studying sports fan violence using qualitative strategies that I have labeled "intensive case history analysis." The reader should be able to use these ideas to study most incidents of sports fan violence. Chapter 4 tells the reader about the structural and demographic conditions under which fan violence takes place and about the persons who are likely to carry out this violence. Chapter 5 presents research questions and a theory of socialization to understand how fans are socialized to be violent.

Chapter 6 looks at two major incidents of fan violence in the United States—the celebrating riots at Ohio State in 2002 and in Boston after the Red Sox victory over the Yankees in 2004. This chapter is based on a theoretical model of celebrating riots that I developed, which uses the intensive case history approach to present the data about the riots. Chapter 7 shows how elements within society manage the tragedies associated with serious fan violence. In particular it examines how Boston sports fans and others dealt with a death linked to the fan violence after the Red Sox riot. Chapter 8 presents and evaluates several solutions that have been proposed for the prevention of sports fan violence, particularly celebrating riots.

Appendix A lists information about serious celebrating riots that have occurred in the United States since 1960, with the idea that these events should be researched by collective behavior scholars. Appendix B reprints recommendations for dealing with celebrating riots developed by the Ohio State University in the aftermath of the 2002 riots. Appendix C reprints my value-added analysis of the Heysel soccer tragedy that occurred in Belgium in 1985.

I began my research on sports fan violence in 1975. Over the years I have written and talked about my research in many media, including scholarly articles, op-ed pieces, newspaper interviews, and radio and television interviews. I decided I wanted to draw these materials into one volume. However, instead of just reprinting my work I have rewritten most of it, adding, where appropriate, new material. Only appendix C is a direct reprint of my previous work.

My research has been aided and supported over the years by many students and friends. In that regard I would like to thank Kim Dugan, Duane Dukes, Sarah Harkness, Bob Hart, Annie Hauser, Mike Kelsey, Pat Payne, Mike Puleo, Desiree Rodriguez, Mike Veneman, Rusty Ward, Terri Weaver, and several generations of collective behavior students who helped me with my newspaper research. Two sport sociologists, Michael Malmisur and the late Mike Smith, gave me considerable guidance about the place of sport in America.

Clark McPhail of the University of Illinois has been an inspiration to me over the years. While he will not agree with all that is said in this book, he has greatly contributed to whatever insights I have about the social problem of fan violence.

Alan McClare and Melissa McNitt of Rowman & Littlefield have been very supportive throughout this project.

My wife, Diane, has been of great assistance during this research, not only through her capacities as an academic wife and teacher in her own right, but also as a professional editor. I am deeply appreciative of her help and support over the years.

References

U.S. Department of Education. 2003. *Report of the Proceedings*. National Conference Addressing Issues Related to Celebratory Riots. Newton, MA: Higher Education Center for Alcohol and Other Drug Abuse and Violence Prevention.

Wann, D. L., M. J. Melnick, G. W. Russell, and D. G. Pease. 2001. *Sport Fans: The Psychology and Social Impact of Spectators*. New York: Routledge.

2

Sports Fan Violence: An Overview

A sports riot is defined as violence—vandalism, throwing missiles, rushing the field or court, committing arson, and/or fighting—committed by five or more individuals in a crowd of at least one hundred people associated with a formally organized sporting event. Any one of these violent behaviors committed by five or more individuals is a sufficient condition to define an event as fan violence or a sports riot.

Sporting events remain one of the prime reasons for groups to gather in the United States (from professional football down to local community softball games). The increase in attendance at sporting events in the United States since 1960 has been phenomenal. In 1960, attendance at regular season professional baseball was over nineteen million, and by 2003 it was over sixty-seven million (Tomasch 2004). Attendance in other major sports has increased as well. The National Football League reports that the attendance in 1960 was over three million, and by 2003 it was over seventeen million. The National Basketball

This chapter is a revision of parts of Jerry M. Lewis, "Fan Violence: An American Social Problem," in *Research in Social Problems and Public Policy*, ed. M. Lewis, vol. 2, 175–206 (Greenwich, CT: JAI Press, 1982). Used with the kind permission of Elsevier Press.

Association figures show similar patterns, with the attendance in 1960–1961 at over one million, and by 2002–2003 it was over twenty million. University and college football attendances have shown considerable increases as well.

Sometimes at these sporting events, fan violence occurs. The social determinants of such episodes of collective behavior are often alluded to, lamented, and even deplored, but systematic behavioral analysis of these episodes has not been adequately pursued. Charles Page, a leading authority in the sociology of sport, has written that few scholars have applied their skills to the study of particularly dramatic, and often traumatic, events in the world of sport. He writes, "certain events, given the mass dimensions of modern sport and the keen widespread interest it invokes, take on 'crisis' or 'revolutionary' character" (Talamini and Page 1973, 9).

This book argues that fan violence is a social problem in North America that should be of concern to its citizens. Neil J. Smelser (1997, 18) proposes that modern sociology has drawn three intellectual outlooks, which he labels the natural-scientific, humanistic, and artistic orientations. The natural-scientific is represented by evidence showing which and why individuals get involved in fan violence. The humanistic deals with the harm to individuals and sport in general that is caused by fan violence. The artistic tradition is represented primarily by chapters 7 and 8, which show how people respond to serious fan violence (7) and solutions to fan violence (8).

This chapter presents two theoretical explanations for why fan violence occurs. They are Smelser's value-added theory and McPhail's categories of crowd behavior. Both theories are based in the collective behavior literature.

Smelser's Theory of Collective Behavior

Neil J. Smelser (1962) argues that the explanation of violence lies in social problems ingrained in the fabric of society. Smelser's theory is useful because of its comprehensive approach to collective violence, particularly fan violence. Smelser's value-added model is a general approach to collective behavior events, particularly hostile outbursts. In building a background it should be made clear that the basis of Smelser's ideas is greatly influenced by the work of Talcott Parsons, Edward Shils, and R. F. Bales (cf. Smelser 1962, 23–24). It is particularly important to link the place of values in Parsonian theory with ideas of the generalized beliefs in Smelser's model. Thus, any discussion of the determinants should include the "components of social action" on which the six (five) determinants are based. These components are labeled in the Parsonian system of thought as values, norms, roles, and situational facilities. These ideas are most clearly presented by Parsons (1961, 30–79) in his essay in *Theories of Society*. Placing Smelser's thought in the context of general social theory would help to alleviate the seemingly ad hoc origin of the categories that many of the discussions in present texts imply. The inclusion of the components would inform the student of the theoretical links between Smelser's work and that of Talcott Parsons, which, for purposes of educating students concerning sociological theory in general, is most desirable. Such linking could also aid the student to think about how other theories in collective behavior (indeed, theories in general) began and how people try to "piece together" bits and scraps of what is known in the attempt to explain what is unknown.

Smelser's model is divided into five determinants, each with a set of subdeterminants. The determinants are (1) structural conduciveness, (2) structural strain, (3) growth of a generalized belief, (4) mobilization for action, and (5) social control. The precipitating event which some versions of the Smelser model use is treated under the growth of generalized belief.

Structural Conduciveness

This determinant refers to conditions of social structure which describe structural possibilities for an incident of collective behavior to happen. Structural conduciveness sets the parameters and constraints for the other components of the model, particularly structural strain in the context of conduciveness. The model relates conduciveness to several subdeterminants: "The structure of responsibility in situations strain; the presence channels for expressing grievances; the possibility of communication among the aggrieved" (Smelser 1962, 227).

In reference to conduciveness and these subdeterminants, the researcher should attempt to discover whether the participants in the hostile outburst could identify someone or some event that was responsible, whether there were appropriate channels for expressing grievances, and whether the aggrieved had an opportunity to communicate with each other.

In relation to sports riots it becomes necessary to determine if fans believe that someone is responsible for the failure of their team to win. This might include players, coaches, or referees. Further, it should be determined if the fans feel that there are channels for expressing their grievances.

Structural Strain

This determinant falls within conduciveness. The researcher is asked to look particularly at values and norms to see if they are a source of strain. It asks the analyst to determine if the sports riot is tied to a larger community problem (value strain) or to the sporting event itself (normative strain).

Growth of a Generalized Belief

Smelser's model instructs the researcher to look for beliefs which guide action. Hostile beliefs are rooted in ambiguity and anxiety derived from conditions of strain (Smelser 1962, 102). These beliefs become shared (generalized) in terms of three issues: who the responsible agents are, whether they should be punished, and whether rioters will escape sanctions for their actions (omnipotence). The notion of the generalized belief is a key variable in Smelser's formulation. In regard to sports riots it requires that one locate a set of beliefs or attitudes that have served to direct the behavior of the sports fans as they attempt to assess blame.

Mobilization for Action

Here the scholar looks at the subdeterminants of a hostile outburst, including leadership, as well as the initial and derived phases of the outburst. Most incidents of collective behavior change during the flow of events. Smelser refers to this as the process of moving from the initial and derived phases. The question for the analyst is whether the sports riot begins for reasons related to more general social conditions of the game per se and shifts for reasons related to social control. For example, the police or National Guard may become the focal point of the riot if they use force deemed inappropriate by the rioters.

Social Control

The Smelser model proposes that the researcher look at several dimensions of social control that shape a hostile outburst and prevent it from getting out of hand. Under social control the scholar studies issues of formal control from traditional sources, such as the police, and informal social control, from sources such as marshals or ministers. The implications of Smelser's model for sports riots research is that any explanation of such a riot should be based on variables which explain the riot as a hostile expression of underlying strains and grievances.

It will be shown in chapter 4 that the "strain" aspect of the Smelser model probably does not apply to celebrating fan violence. However, understanding the model is important for two reasons. First, it is useful for organizing a variety of data when using the intensive case method that is presented in the next chapter. Second, my theory of celebrating violence, a subset of Smelser's theory, is presented in chapter 6. Smelser's theory is the logical predecessor of my celebrating riot approach to spectator violence.

McPhail's Model of Categories of Behavior

Clark McPhail, of the University of Illinois, is a leading researcher on collective behavior.[1] McPhail (1991), writing in the symbolic interaction tradition, argues that a crowd violence re-searcher must be clear on the variables that he or she is studying when looking at sports fan violence. McPhail's approach is not a theory of fan violence per se. Rather, it is a theory of what indi-viduals do in crowds. It is necessary for the researcher to apply McPhail's ideas to sports riots by showing how the categories help us understand the behavior of violent sports fans. His ideas can be linked to both Smelser's approach and my approach (see chapter 6) to sports riots. The categories help clarify what Smelser means by *mobilization for action*, while in reference to my approach to fan violence, the McPhail categories are particularly useful for looking at the behavior of sports fans when they are either rushing the field or floor after a victory or celebrating at a national urban gathering place. Some of the important charac-teristics of individuals involved in fan violence situations are discussed in the following pages.

McPhail conducted a number of research projects and re-views of the literature where he brought into question the expla-nations of crowd behavior made by collective behavior scholars. One of his main concerns has been the failure of these scholars to adequately show exactly what they are attempting to explain. McPhail has suggested that if scholars did not know what the dependent variables were, they could not define what the inde-pendent variables were or how they influenced the dependent variables.

McPhail (1991) has developed thirty-four categories of be-havior that purport to describe the activities of crowd members in any crowd. These categories have been developed theoreti-cally and empirically by McPhail and his graduate students.

As can be seen in figure 2.1, the categories are divided into seven major groups, including collective orientation, vocaliza-tion, verbalization, gesticulation, vertical locomotion, horizontal locomotion, and manipulation.

Collective Orientation

This category refers to the classification of orientation to-ward direction. McPhail (1991) argues that collective orientation

Collective Orientation	Collective Vocalization	Collective Verbalization
1. Clustering	1. Ooh-aah-oohing	1 Chanting
2. Arcing/ringing	2. Yeaing	2. Singing
3. Gazing/facing	3. Booing	3. Praying
4. Vigiling	4. Whistling	4. Reciting
	5. Hissing	5. Pledging
	6. Wailing	
	7. Laughing	

Collective Gesticulation
(nonverbal symbols)

1. Roman salute (arm extended forward, palm down, fingers together)
2. Solidarity salute (closed fist raised above the shoulder level)
3. Digitus Obscenus (fist raised, middle finger extended)
4. #1 (fist raised, index finger and middle fingers separated and extended)
5. Peace (fist raised, index finger and middle fingers separated and extended)
6. Praise or victory (both arms fully extended overhead)

Collective Vertical Locomotion	Collective Horizontal Locomotion	Collective Manipulation
1. Sitting	1. Pedestrian clustering	1. Applauding
2. Standing	2. Queuing	2. Synchro-clapping
3. Jumping	3. Surging	3. Finger-snapping
4. Bowing	4. Marching	4. Grasping, lifting, waving object
5. Kneeling	5. Jogging	5. Grasping, lifting, throwing object
6. Kowtowing	6. Running	6. Grasping, lifting, pushing object

Figure 2.1. *Some Elementary Forms of Collective Behavior in Common*

is a rough indicator of a range of objects to which individuals in the crowd (*gatherings* in McPhail's terms) might be giving attention. Collective orientation is made up of four subcategories: clustering, arcing/ringing, gazing/facing, and vigiling. *Clustering* refers to a process where from two to six individuals have a common or convergent direction of attention. In the stands, it is possible to observe small groups of baseball fans all orienting themselves in the same direction, though not necessarily in the direction of the game. McPhail notes that there are also pedestrian and conversation clusters.

Arcing/ringing refers to the process where small groups of people create an arc or a ring around a focal point. Typically clustering and arcing/ringing go hand in hand. The arcing/ringing process is done in concert with clustering. For example, when police or ushers go into the stands to stop a fight, one can observe this arcing/ringing process as individuals attempt to observe the action.

Gazing/facing and *vigiling* describe the direction people are looking. These rarely happen at sporting events, although on occasion one might see vigiling at a crucial turning point in the sporting event, such as a field goal to resolve a tie where both teams' fans assume an expectant stance before the kick.

Collective Vocalization

This is the process where two or more persons engage in common vocal sounds. McPhail (1991) defines subcategories of behavior under collective vocalization, including ooh-aah-oohing, yeaing, booing, whistling, hissing, laughing, and wailing. *Ooh-aahing* is often heard at football games when a long punt is kicked with a beautiful spiral. *Yeaing* is cheering. Of course, *booing* is a staple of all sporting events, particularly in the evaluation of an umpire's or referee's decision or a perceived infraction by a player, such as hitting a batter after a homerun in baseball, and is often associated with chanting, which is discussed shortly. *Whistling* is rarely seen at American sporting events, although it happens at some English soccer matches in a very unique manner. The winning team's supporters will begin to whistle to encourage the referee to end the match. In contrast to American sport, the timekeeper is the referee on the pitch who ends the match with three short whistle blasts.

Hissing and *wailing* are rarely seen at American sporting events, but *laughing* is often seen in regard to the antics of team mascots, such as the San Diego (baseball) Chicken, or at the behavior of fans in certain sections of a football stadium, like the "Dawg Pound" associated with the Cleveland Browns.

Collective Verbalization

This category describes two or more people engaged in co-ordinated vocal sounds (but not speech). McPhail (1991) notes several subcategories of collective vocalization, including chanting, singing, praying, reciting, and pledging." English football matches have much more chanting and singing than in the United States, where, for the most part, *singing* is reserved for the National Anthem. *Chanting* is usually done either as a derisive statement against a referee's decision, as in "Bullshit, bullshit," or as a supporting statement saying a player's name, as in "Barry (Bond), Barry." *Praying, reciting,* and *pledging* rarely happen at American sporting events.

Collective Gesticulation

Collective gesticulation occurs when two or more persons coordinate their physical gestures. This is often done in connection with collective vocalization and verbalization. McPhail (1991) describes six types of collective gesticulation, including the Roman salute; the solidarity salute; digitus obscenus; and the peace, praise, or victory signs. Two categories of gesticulations occur most often at American sporting events: digitus obscenus and praise or victory signs. *Digitus obscenus,* or giving someone the middle finger, is done to opposing players by groups of fans who want to challenge or criticize some action by the player. For example, this can occur during basketball games when an opposing player does some action that is defined as showboating. The *victory sign* is used when one's team scores a goal or run. This is usually accompanied by high fives with other fans.

Collective Vertical Locomotion

Collective vertical locomotion refers to coordinated vertical behavior involving two or more crowd members. McPhail (1991) delineates six types of behaviors: sitting, standing, jumping, bowing, kneeling, and kowtowing. The latter four seldom happen at such events, while *sitting* and *standing* are typical patterns at American sporting events.

Collective Horizontal Locomotion

Collective horizontal locomotion takes place when two or more people coordinate their movements in space. McPhail (1991) proposes six types of collective horizontal movement: pedestrian clustering, queuing, surging, marching, jogging, and running. The latter four behaviors seldom happen at American sporting events.

When the stands are not completely filled, you can observe small groups of supporters moving back and forth in *pedestrian clusters*. For American sports spectators, *queuing* happens at toilet facilities or refreshment lines.

Collective Manipulation

Collective manipulation describes the process of two or more people coordinating their hand activities. McPhail (1991) defines six categories of collective manipulation: applauding; synchro-clapping; finger-snapping; grasping, lifting, waving object; grasping, lifting, throwing object; and grasping, lifting, pushing object. *Applause* is seen at many American sporting events, including tennis, after a good point; in football, when an injured player leaves the field; or in track and field, when a successful individual effort, such as a winning long jump, has happened.

Desmond Morris (1981, 259–60) has a very complex description of *synchro-clapping* in English soccer which is useful to our understanding in American sport. It happens in four different ways: (1) to welcome the team on to the field at the start of the match, (2) to provide a beat for the songs, (3) to encourage players to speed up their play, and (4) to encourage players to perform in a more interesting manner. In American sport, synchro-clapping takes place when fans want to encourage players to continue to rally in baseball or to play defense in basketball.

Grasping, lifting, waving objects is an important part of fan behavior at basketball games when fans will be encouraged to wave wands or placards as the opposing player is shooting a free throw. This is supposed to encourage the opposing player to miss the free throw, and it is also an indication of positive fan support. *Grasping, lifting, throwing objects* rarely occurs in coordination, and usually involves the throwing of objects such as beer cans, batteries, or other types of debris at outfielders in baseball or at exiting players or officials in football. *Grasping, lifting, pushing objects* is demonstrated by American fans following championship victories. For example, fans have been known to grasp and overturn cars in celebratory riots (McPhail 1991, 170; Lewis 1982).

Complex Collective Behavior in Common

Although McPhail describes his behavior categories as separate entities, he emphasizes that these elementary forms of collective behavior rarely happen alone. Typically they occur in some system of combination. He writes, "People frequently engage in two or more of these behaviors that are performed in the same direction or at the same tempo or velocity, or are otherwise judged common to the two or more persons on one or more of these dimensions" (McPhail 1991, 171).

Understanding this behavior is important because fans who riot before, during, or after a sporting event typically draw on a repertoire of behaviors that are used in a normal sporting event. That is, in carrying out a riot, these individuals often use the same behaviors as normal or typical fans at a sporting event. Therefore the analyst should be looking for these behaviors in a systematic way, either through participant observation (the method that McPhail prefers) or through photographs and films (see chapter 3).

In concluding this section, let's look at how the categories of behavior that McPhail has delineated might be seen in a celebrating sports riot. My description of the riot does not refer to any particular riot but is, in a sense, an ideal type based on my research and field experiences both in the United States and in England.

The typical celebrating sports riot is located either on the playing field or the court after the winning of a championship.

The other venue is a natural urban gathering place, often near the home field or court of the winning team.

When fans begin to gather in a natural urban gathering site after a victory, it is possible to see the McPhail categories develop. One can observe, at a minimum, a combination chanting, gesturing, and pedestrian clustering as fans begin to move through the streets expressing their excitement and joy over the winning of the championship by their team. This, in itself, does not constitute a sports riot, but can lead to one. The celebration can move to vandalism as the fans continue their activity. New categories are often added as it is possible to see applauding and cheering as the fans become destructive. The vandalism is often minor at this point, including breaking windows and street lights and turning over mailboxes and trash cans.

Sometimes the vandalism escalates to arson with the burning of trash cans, debris in the streets, and cars or emergency response vehicles. When the attack on cars and trucks begins, the additional categories of grasping, lifting, pushing, and victory gestures appear. In this attack on automobiles it would be possible to see at least five or six of the McPhail categories being executed during the riot.

After serious vandalism begins, the police often move against the rioters with tear gas and other physical force. This is where fighting begins between rioters and police. In this phase of the celebrating riot, the new behaviors seen include digitus obscenus and running, although the other behaviors mentioned could also be present.

In summary, scholars are instructed by the McPhail categories to take a careful look at the behaviors that they are trying to explain. In a 2004 paper, McPhail, Schweingruber, and Ceobanu proposed an expanded and revised version of his theory. They argued, based on systematic observation of a Promise Keepers rally on the Mall involving over one-half million people, that scholars should look for forty-five categories of behavior. These behaviors are grouped into four basic categories, including body position, facing, voicing, and manipulating. Even though these forty-five categories are based on the emergent activities of a peaceful crowd, they provide the scholar of sports riots useful tools for describing the behavior of violent fans. This is true for either participant observation research on violent fans or studying behavior in photographs and films. In the next chapter, I discuss how sociologists should go about studying crowds using the theoretical models presented in this chapter.

Note

1. This section is a revision of pages 161–67 in J. M. Lewis and A. Scarisbrick-Hauser, "An Analysis of Football Crowd Safety Reports Using the McPhail Categories," in *Football, Violence and Social Identity*, ed. R. Giulianotti, N. Bonney, and M. Hepworth (London: Routledge, 1994), chap. 7.

References

Lewis, J. M. 1982. "Fan Violence: An American Social Problem." In *Research in Social Problems and Public Policy*, ed. M. Lewis, vol. 2, 175–206. Greenwich, CT: JAI Press.

Lewis, J. M., and A. Scarisbrick-Hauser. 1994. "An Analysis of Football Crowd Safety Reports Using the McPhail Categories." In *Football, Violence and Social Identity*, ed. R. Giulianotti, N. Bonney, and M. Hepworth, chap. 7. London: Routledge.

McPhail, C. 1991. *The Myth of the Madding Crowd*. New York: Aldine de Gruyter.

McPhail, C., D. Schweingruber, and A. Ceobanu. 2004. "Alternating and Varying Collective Actions in a Temporary Setting." Paper presented at the annual American Sociological Association meeting, San Francisco, CA.

Morris, D. 1981. *The Soccer Tribe*. London: Jonathan Cape.

Parsons, T. 1961. *Theories of Society*. Glencoe, NY: The Free Press.

Smelser, N. J. 1962. *Theory of Collective Behavior*. New York: The Free Press.

Smelser, N. J. 1997. *Problematics in Sociology: The Georg Simmel Lectures*. Berkeley: The University of California Press.

Talamini, J. T., and C. H. Page, eds. 1973. *Sports and Society: An Anthology*. Boston: Little, Brown & Company.

Tomasch, K. 2004. "Baseball Attendance." kenn.com.

3

Approaches to Studying Sports Fan Violence

This chapter develops a protocol for the analysis of violent sports crowds. It argues that the study of fan violence should be theoretically informed and methodologically grounded. It describes the primary and secondary sources that can be used in the study of sports fan violence, particularly when the investigator is not present when the violence happens.

I call my methodology for the study of sports crowds, particularly violent crowds, "intensive case histories." It is intensive because the approach uses a number of data sources in trying to understand what happens in a violent sports crowd. It is a case history because I tend to focus on sports crowd incidents that have a clear beginning and end. I have used this approach for many years, developing it when I did a study of the 1970 Kent State shootings (Lewis 1972) and extending it in my study of the Heysel Stadium riot and crowd crush in Belgium (Lewis 1989; see appendix C).

Scholars should approach fan violence with a triangulation strategy. Triangulation is developed using primary and secondary sources. The sources include site visits, personal interviews, newspaper stories, photographs, and police documents. Studies from the United States and England are used to illustrate the protocol.

Sporting events can lead to violent outbursts by segments of spectators resulting in serious injuries or death. Since sporting events remain one of the prime reasons for groups to gather in public, it becomes essential to understand outbursts of violence that may be associated with these events.

Very seldom, however, is the investigator present when fan violence happens. Therefore, the sociologist must approach the study in such a way that a wide variety of data can be used in the analysis.

There seem to be two basic approaches to an incident of fan violence: the survey approach and the collective behavior approach. In the survey approach, after an incident of fan violence has happened, the sociologist undertakes an investigation of an individual's response to the incident. The questions range over a variety of issues, including what caused the riot and what types of harm the riot will bring to the institutions, either a college, a university, or a professional sports team. While this approach certainly has merit and contributes to our understanding of fan violence, it is generally focused on the short- and long-term consequences of the rioting, not the actual incident itself.

In contrast, the collective behavior approach to fan violence looks at the incident per se, bringing a wide variety of resources to bear on efforts to understand what happened in the riot. Since I write in the collective behavior tradition, my strategy is to use the protocol that follows. After reviewing each data source in the protocol, I show how the source can be linked to the three theoretical models presented in chapter 2. The chapter concludes with suggestions for how the scholar can study social control forces using a triangulation strategy.

The Protocol

First, there is a general discussion of methodological triangulation.[1] This is followed by a description of various methods that can be used in gathering data about sports crowd violence.

Triangulation

The idea of triangulation is that multiple methods provide a more adequate database than a single method (Webb et al. 1966). This is particularly true when one is researching a problem that is difficult to study, such as sports crowd violence. In addition, multiple methods are needed in the study of crowd violence since the investigator is rarely present when the violence occurs.

There are two types of methodological triangulation. The "within method" encourages the sociologist to use varieties of the same method, while the "between method" suggests that distinct methodological approaches are needed in the research. This discussion places its emphasis on between-method triangulation. Two assumptions govern this discussion of methodology. First, the methodology should be grounded theoretically. This chapter does this using two theories proposed in the previous chapter—Smelser's general model and McPhail's categories. Second, the protocol should be relatively easy to use since opportunities to study sports crowd violence, or any crowd violence, often come to sociologists who are not trained in collective behavior theory or methods. Indeed, many nonsociologists, such as journalists or referees, are present at sports crowd violence when the sociologist is not. This protocol is designed to be "user friendly" so that any thoughtful person can analyze sports crowd violence in a systematic manner

Data Sources for Studying Sports Crowd Violence

There are five sources of data that can be used to investigate sports riots. These include site visits, personal interviews, newspaper accounts, photographs, and police documents. I describe each source and show how they are linked to the two theoretical models presented in chapter 2. Because the Smelser model is so complex, I have provided, in figure 3.1, a summary linking the Smelser determinants to the data sources. Figure 3.1 shows the twenty-five cells a researcher needs to deal with when using the approach advocated in this book. This presents a formidable, but

	Smelser's Model Data Sources				
Determinants	Site Visitation	Personal Interviews	Newspaper Accounts	Photographs/ Films	Police Documents
Structural Conduciveness	Excellent	Excellent	Excellent	Good	Poor
Structural Strain	Good	Excellent	Fair	Good	Poor
Generalized Belief	Poor	Excellent	Fair	Poor	Poor
Mobilization for Action	Fair	Excellent	Fair	Excellent	Fair
Social Control	Good	Excellent	Poor	Fair	Excellent

Figure 3.1.   A Protocol for the Analysis of Sports Crowd Violence

not impossible challenge. I have classified each source as excellent, good, fair, or poor. *Excellent* means that the data source always generates information that allows the investigator to decide whether the determinant was present or not at the episode of collective behavior. *Good* means the data are almost always present; *fair* means that the investigator has a fifty-fifty chance of getting data relevant to a particular determinant; *poor* indicates a less than fifty-fifty chance of getting data from the particular source in terms of the relevant determinant.

To illustrate the linkages between the two theoretical models and the data sources, I describe my experiences conducting research in the United States and, occasionally, I include examples from my research on English football (soccer) fan violence.

Site Visits

Rarely does the sociologist happen to be at the scene of sports crowd violence. Thus, he or she is forced to reconstruct the riot behavior. When visiting the scene of a riot, the investigator should do so not only when a crowd is present, but when the stadium is empty. When a crowd is present, it is possible to capture the conditions that may have led to the violence. For example, crowd noise, fan movement, and location of the police all might be factors in the riot. However, a visit to the stadium when it is empty of fans is also useful. It allows one to move around to achieve the point of view of fans, both violent and nonviolent, as well as police, players, and vendors.

Second, fan violence happens in locations other than the stadium, and visiting these sites is also useful. For example, sports violence generally happens in or near the stadium, but it can occur in the center of a major city or, as in England, in railroad stations. Whatever the location, a site visit is crucial to the data collection protocol.

In regard to the Smelser model (see figure 3.1), site visits are an excellent source of data for structural conduciveness, which refers to situations generated by the social structure that provide a range of possibilities within which a hostile outburst can occur. Site visits also help the researcher understand, in a limited way, the growth of a generalized belief and mobilization for action. This determinant describes those conditions that are permissive for sports violence to occur. Of particular interest is whether fans identify someone for the winning or losing of the game or match and whether fans can share their feelings with others at the sporting event.

Site visits are useful because they allow the investigator to determine, first, whether fans could interact with each other as well as social control forces. That is, do fans have physical and verbal access to each other? Both theoretical models assume that the actors in the crowd will have some form of verbal and visual access to one another.

In the Smelser model, this is particularly important for the determinant of mobilization for action. Mobilization suggests that individuals will be coordinating their activities. A site visit is less important to the understanding of the McPhail categories after the fact of the crowd action, but very important if the investigator can be present during the incident.

Second, a site visit allows the investigator the opportunity to determine whether fans have easy or difficult access to the playing field. The site visit allows the sociologist to study the range of movement possible in the violence. In United States stadia, sports fans have easier access to the field than do English soccer fans. The reason for this is that one of the responses to soccer hooligans in England has been the construction of fences and other barriers around the playing pitch. To be sure, some playing fields in the United States can be reached with minimal effort, while others are more difficult. For example, fans have easy access to the field at Wrigley Field (Cubs), Chicago, and Fenway Park (Red Sox), Boston. Thus, play could be quickly interrupted with a field invasion or missiles thrown from the stands. In contrast, fans do not have as easy an access to Jacobs Field (Indians) in Cleveland.

Scholars need to use their imagination in getting access to sites. One of my students went to the Internet for his research and was able to get solid photographs of the sites associated with the crowds in the running of the bulls in Pamplona, Spain.

Personal Interviews

As you can see from figure 3.1, personal interviews are the best source of information on fan violence. Yet, they are often difficult to obtain. Consequently, the sociologist using personal interviews should remember to cast his or her net broadly. Obvious candidates for interviews are violent and nonviolent fans, police, ushers, and sportscasters. However, there are other interview sources. For example, vendors are often closer to the crowd action than anyone else. Indeed, some may actually be targets of the riot behavior. Another source of interviews is people who live in the area where the violence happened. They often have unique vantage points to observe the violence. However, it should be remembered that these people may be quite angry about what has happened to them, and they are frustrated by the fact they have had to deal with rioters at their front door.

Personal interviews are used in reference to structural conduciveness to determine whether winning or losing was a factor in the riot. This can be determined by talking with the fans who rioted as well as those who did not. Referees are also useful interviewees on this question.

Newspaper Accounts

Sociologists often use newspapers as well as magazine stories in their studies of crowds. This is certainly appropriate. Generally, journalists who write about fan violence are present when the violence takes place. Journalists are trained observers who can articulate their experiences. While their accounts are useful, there are some difficulties that should be noted. First, journalists rarely report the gender or race of individuals involved in crowds. Newspaper and magazine accounts tend to describe the size of the crowd or the total numbers arrested, and they usually refer to categories of people in terms such as fans, spectators, or hooligans. Second, journalists do not take into account those who do not riot, choosing to write about the violent fans and not those who act in verbal support of the rioters or those who were simply acting as observers of the violence. Third, journalists tend to describe the crowd as a total unit behaving in concert. Seldom do journalistic accounts describe the variety of behavior that is present in any crowd.

The use of newspapers will probably continue as a major source of data because of the difficulty involved in anticipating when an incident of fan violence is going to take place so that one might be present as an investigator at the riot. However, Danzger warns us that there can be biases built into the data because of the fact that most conflict data are reported by the wire services (United Press International, Associated Press). He adds, "Reports of the occurrence of an event and many elements of description, such as the number and type of participants, the actions occurring and so forth may be accepted as fact. Given the structure of corrective processes, such facts are more likely to be valid if gathered for a time sequence rather than for a single event" (Danzger 1975, 581).

Earl and colleagues (2004) extended the ideas of Danzger by describing in some detail two biases that influence the use of the newspaper and magazine sources for the study of crowds. The first is called selection bias. The authors write, "Newspaper data suffer from selection bias because news agencies do not report on all events that actually occur. Critics claim that the sample of events on which newspapers do report is not representative but is instead structured by various factors such as competition over newspaper space, reporting norms, and editorial concerns" (Earl et al. 2004, 68–69). I think that riots associated with nonchampionship play may be underreported, as well as those associated with competition at the high school level versus collegiate or professional sport.

The second bias is called description bias and refers to the truth of newspaper reports. Earl and colleagues (2004, 73), in evaluating description bias, write, "Although newspaper data may ignore key dimensions of a protest (e.g., its purpose), when event characteristics are included, especially hard news items, the reports are, in general, accurate." The analyses of these writers for sport sociologists studying fan violence suggests that we should be on the alert for the omission of some riot events from our samples.

In using the newspapers as a "running record" (Smith 1978) of violence, scholars should go beyond the simple recording of an act of violence and deal with its severity. Newspaper accounts provide information on the fans' reaction to winning and losing and can be used to support personal interviews. In addition, newspaper accounts can provide information about events during the game. For example, reactions of the fans to a crucial referee's decision may be in a newspaper account. Press reporters are generally reliable about the behavior of the rioters but are poor sources of information about who did the behavior. Reporters in both print and electronic journalism have a tendency to describe violent fans with such limited terms as thugs, hooligans, bums, and "not true fans."

In the United States, newspapers can be used as sources of data about riots at the high school, collegiate, and professional levels of competition. Reporting is regional as there is no national newspaper in the United States as there is in England. *USA Today* is an exception to this statement, but rarely reports riot data. In order to get a national picture of sports violence in the United States, the researcher must work with a number of papers, including regional papers such as the *St. Louis Post-Dispatch* or Cleveland's *Plain Dealer*. Most researchers use the

New York Times for riot data because of its accessibility in libraries nationwide, as well as its excellent index. However, the *Times*'s coverage is incomplete. The *New York Times* is also the best American source for data on English soccer hooliganism, but it is still incomplete.

Newspapers are excellent sources for structural conduciveness because the research can generate information about the importance of the game in terms of championship play. Newspapers are less valuable for the other determinants in the Smelser model because the information is generally not as detailed as the scholar would hope for, particularly with regard to social control. Newspapers do not appear to be an important source of data for using the McPhail categories.

Photographs and Films

Photographs as well as films are used for looking at the behavior of fans, particularly in the context of spatial relationships. It is difficult to infer motive from these sources. Photographs provide evidence about the types of behavior that occur at a sports riot, but not frequency, since photographs rarely achieve anything resembling a random sample. Films are better sources of data about behavior because of the continuous record, but they are much less available to researchers. In studying photographs and films, the researcher should be aware that not all riot behavior is hostile. Indeed, many rioters are joyous even when they are committing vandalism such as tearing down goalposts.

Photographs provide clues to the reaction of fans at the moment of winning or losing. Photographs are helpful in analyzing winning or losing in relation to celebrating or punishing riots. Indeed one of the ironies of fan violence is that destructive behavior is often joyously conducted because of happy circumstances—winning the game. Often the focus of a photographer is an individual rather than a group, but sometimes one is lucky enough to locate photographs with a sociological bent—that is, one that shows large groups responding to a win or loss. Many photographs are unpublished, and the sociologist should contact photographers directly for additional materials. Photographs are an outstanding source of data for behavior because they can be classified easily into the topology categories, but they are not good sources for describing the extent of that behavior. Photographs are also helpful for identifying age, gender, and race of rioters and nonrioters. In some cases sweatshirts and T-shirts can provide additional clues to the background of the fans because of team identification such as names or mascots that are printed on the shirts.

The basic difference between American and English published photographs is the point of view that editors want to communicate about the fan violence. American editors print large crowd pictures while their English counterparts seem to favor pictures of small groups of soccer fans. Of course, both types are needed for adequate representation of the riot. Rarely do American or English papers print photographs of nonrioting fans responding negatively to rioting fans.

Police Documents

Documents from the police are good sources for the behavior of individual arrested fans but, as noted before, rarely provide information on group behavior. In addition, police documents may be used to determine where police were before the fan violence happened. If major violence does take place, it is likely—in both the United States and Britain—that an internal investigation will be conducted. The findings of the investigation are usually presented in a report, but the researcher must use tact and care in getting access and using the report.

In the United States, police seem to be less sensitive to public criticism than in England; hence, they are not always willing to show materials to researchers. In England, police are more concerned with public attitudes, and this often gets translated into a willingness to work with scholars studying policing problems including crowd control. Nevertheless, getting access in both countries takes considerable time and patience but is generally worth the effort. There are three types of police documents that are helpful to the sociologist. First, there are planning documents, which describe the amount, type, and location of police being used to control a sporting event. For example, this document tells the researcher where dog teams were located prior, during, and after a sporting event.

Second, there is the police arrest report. This is the form used to record the basic facts of the arrest and is often the source information for a subsequent trial. However, the sociologist is not always able to get access to these reports. When this access is obtained, these forms are good on demographic data such as age, sex, race, and residence. These documents provide information on individual behavior but rarely describe group behavior. That is, it is virtually impossible to infer crowd behavior from individual arrest reports. In using arrest reports the researcher has the obligation to protect the person arrested from public exposure. It should be remembered that arrest does not mean conviction.

Third, there may be internal reports after a major episode of fan violence. This is usually a detailed report and is very helpful to the scholar. However, it is generally not easy to obtain, though the researcher should try.

Police documents are useful sources of data about conduciveness when coupled with personal interviews. For example, they can provide information on the history of the relationship between the teams; that is, police documents can tell the investigator whether the fans of the two teams have had conflict before, either in previous seasons or in earlier meetings during the present season. Police documents are also useful in determining when the violence began, thus allowing the investigator the chance to link the analysis into the dynamics of the game or match, particularly in reference to winning or losing. In both the United States and England, arrest data usually provide age, gender, race, and residence, but seldom provide detailed information on occupation.

In the next section, I present a case history showing how to use the protocol when combined with the Smelser model to study fan violence.

An Illustrative Intensive Case History

On Sunday, December 16, 2001, a sports riot took place in Cleveland, Ohio, at the end of the National Football League game between the Cleveland Browns and the Jacksonville Jaguars.

This riot was a major sports riot for several reasons. First, it altered the game. Second, it resulted in policy changes. Third, it generated considerable regional and national news coverage. Fourth, it involved a considerable number of football fans. Estimates of the number of participants range from seven hundred to one thousand fans. Lastly, the initial response of the Browns' senior management was deemed very inappropriate by a wide number of people. Essentially, the Browns said it was not very serious. One person said that it "wasn't World War II out there."

The impact of this riot can be measured in media interest. It was mentioned on several national television news programs including *CBS News*, *ABC News*, and ESPN's *Sports Center*. The *New York Times* ran two stories on the riot.

Interestingly enough, the riot received widespread cartoon attention, including, for example, the following newspapers: *Akron Beacon Journal*, *Arizona Republic*, *Cincinnati Post*, *Dayton Daily News*, and *USA Today*. One cartoon originating in the *Cincinnati Post* (Stahler 2001) and reprinted in *USA Today* shows two Taliban fighters running from bottles. One fighter asks, "Northern Alliance?" and the other responds, "No, Cleveland Browns Fans!" It also was given considerable regional news attention on radio and television and in newspapers.

Data Sources

I used a number of data sources to study the Cleveland Browns beer bottle riot. All these sources have been discussed above and include site visits, personal interviews, newspaper accounts, photographs and films, and police documents.

In regard to site visits, while I was not at the game when the riot happened, I am familiar with the stadium, having attended a game in the previous season. Also, as a long-term resident of northeastern Ohio I am familiar with the environment of the downtown Cleveland area where the stadium is located.

Personal interviews are important to the investigator, and this riot was no exception. Obvious candidates for interviews include violent and nonviolent football fans, police, ushers, and ticket takers. Ushers and security guards are closest to the fans and can provide a unique perspective on fan concert behavior. There are two types of interviews: one that the scholar completes personally and one that he or she obtains from secondary sources.

For the Cleveland Browns beer bottle riot I interviewed three eyewitnesses to the riot.[2] Afterward, they read the narrative and made suggestions and additions. It should also be noted that I was an "ear witness" to the riot as I listened to the live radio account of Cleveland Browns broadcasters Jim Donovan and Doug Dieken.

Journalists are often present when violence occurs. They provide information about the riots that occur before, during, or after the event. They are helpful in describing the size of the crowd. For this research, I used accounts from four Ohio newspapers: the *Akron Beacon Journal* (2001 [December 18, 23]; Akron area), the *Canton Repository* (2001; Canton area), the *Plain Dealer* (2001 [December 17, 21]; Cleveland area), and the *Record Courier* (2001; Kent area). The first three papers provided material from reporters and photographers at the game, while the last one carried stories from Associated Press reports of the riot.

Photographs can be used to provide clues about the reactions of the fans. They provide evidence about the types of behavior that occur at sports riots. In a few cases, the researcher is also able to obtain films. For this research, I used photographs from newspapers and watched film versions from local and national television reports of the riot.

Police documents are helpful in informing a researcher about the amount and location of officers, how many arrests were made, and the types of violence that occurred.

I was not able to obtain any police documents of the Cleveland Browns beer bottle riot.

I have now reviewed the theory and the data sources. The following analysis combines these two areas of inquiry.

Analysis of the Cleveland Browns Beer Bottle Riot

This analysis uses the Smelser value-added model, including the determinants and the subdeterminants, to order and explain the data about the Cleveland Browns beer bottle riot.

As I noted in chapter 2, any intensive case study of a sports riot should be theoretically framed. A brief review of the model follows. For a more detailed discussion of the value-added model, see chapter 2.

In brief, Smelser's model is divided into five determinants, each with a set of subdeterminants. The determinants are (1) structural conduciveness, (2) structural strain, (3) growth of a generalized belief, (4) mobilization for action, and (5) social control.

The determinant of structural conduciveness refers to conditions of social structure which describe structural possibilities for an incident of collective behavior to happen. Structural conduciveness sets the parameters and constraints for the other components of the model, particularly structural strain, in the context of conduciveness.

Structural strain falls within conduciveness. The researcher looks at values and norms to see if they are sources of strain and determines if the sports riot is tied to a larger community problem (value strain) or to the sporting event itself (normative strain).

Smelser's model instructs the researcher to look for beliefs which guide action. Hostile beliefs are rooted in ambiguity and anxiety derived from conditions of strain (Smelser 1962, 102). These beliefs become shared (generalized) in terms of several issues—who are the responsible agents, should they (the agents) be punished, and will the rioters receive sanctions for their actions (omnipotence)? Under mobilization for action, the scholar looks at the subdeterminants of a hostile outburst, including leadership, as well as the initial and derived phases of the outburst. Most incidents of collective behavior change during the flow of events. Smelser refers to this as the process of moving from the initial to derived phases of the crowd action.

The Smelser model proposes that the researcher look at several dimensions of social control that shape a hostile outburst and prevent it from getting out of hand. Under social control the researcher looks at issues of formal control from traditional sources, such as the police; informal social control, from sources such as marshals or ministers; and normative control. The analysis of the Cleveland Browns beer bottle riot begins with structural conduciveness.

Structural Conduciveness

I used all the data sources to examine structural conduciveness. My knowledge of the site was important because I could determine if the fans thought they could have an impact on officials by throwing bottles. Interviews were also important.

At Cleveland Browns Stadium, the active core was the group of bottle-throwing fans who were protesting the actions of the referee in regard to his instant replay decision. These fans (primarily white males) likely had strong feelings about the referees' decision and its impact on the Browns' playoff chances.

It was clear that the some of the Cleveland Browns fans thought they had no normative way to express their concern over the referee's decision. Many fans booed and expressed disgust for the decision, but some fans decided that this was not an adequate way to protest. One of my interviewees said that if he had had a bottle, he would have thrown it.

In addition, the fans could communicate with each other. To understand the process of communication just before the hostile outburst happened, it is necessary to describe conditions of the Cleveland Browns Stadium. In 2001, it was a new stadium in its third year of use. Sight lines are good and it is possible to see actions of fans in most parts of the stadium. In addition, many fans bring radios so they can hear what sports announcers are saying about the game as well as fan behavior. Thus, it is safe to say that fans had opportunities to communicate with each other.

In summary, all the conditions of structural conduciveness postulated by the Smelser model were met. That is, there was a division of roles so that the active core could carry out the protest. It was possible to blame someone or some act for the decision that was made on the field. Some members of the crowd who protested were able to communicate either orally or visually with other members who were protesting. Here are my data sources for this study.

Structural Strain

To study strain I drew on personal interviews and newspaper accounts. In addition, as an "ear witness" I heard the announcers discussing the referee's decision which affected the outcome of the game. Smelser's model indicates that the analyst should examine strain at the levels of values and norms: Is the sports violence limited to strains located in larger community problems (value strain) or to the sport itself (normative strain)? Let us look at the value question first. The most important value that would have been under strain would be the response to the events of the 9/11 terrorism tragedy. However, there is no evidence to show that 9/11 factor. Other issues of a more general nature that might have influenced the hostile outburst include the economy, unemployment, and racial conflict. Again, there is no evidence indicating that these were factors in the riot.

Strain, then, seems to be more likely at the level of norms. So the analysis turns to normative strain, particularly in relation to the football game. What norms? It was quite clear that the Cleveland fans were hoping that their team's offensive drive would be sustained and lead to a score. Given the time left in the game, this score would have likely been the winning one, thus keeping the Browns in the playoff contention. The first normative strain was the lost opportunity, in the minds of the Browns football fans, to keep in contention for the playoffs.

The second strain was the fans' view that the instant replay should not have been allowed because a subsequent play had already been executed, thereby precluding the replay request. Had the replay been disallowed, the completed pass call would not have been overruled, and the Browns would have continued their drive toward the end zone. After the game, the referee indicated that he had received the request for a replay before the quarterback had snapped the ball. Thus, the replay request was legal in his mind. Interestingly enough, most sports commentators and fans who viewed the replay later agreed that the ball had not been caught and hence it was an incomplete pass. This analysis concludes that there is evidence that normative structural strain was present to facilitate the development of a hostile outburst.

Growth of Generalized Beliefs

Beliefs are difficult to measure in the absence of interviews with those individuals actually doing the rioting. Therefore the analyst must infer beliefs from other sources. I found interviews, newspaper accounts, and photographs the best sources of information.

Smelser argues that certain subdeterminant conditions encourage the development of hostile beliefs. These are labeled ambiguity, anxiety, assigning of responsibility, a desire to punish, and feelings of omnipotence.

Feelings of *ambiguity* were strong among the Browns fans because of the confusion regarding the referee's inappropriate decision about instant replay. These feelings were fueled for those listening to the radio, because both commentators kept remarking on the rule that instant replay could not be used if another play had already been made, which was the case when the Browns' quarterback spiked the ball.

Anxiety was present among the fans because they realized how little time was left on the clock and how important in terms of playoff chances a negative interpretation of the catch would have been. I do not have hard data on this point, but I believe that many fans did not think the catch had been made and were concerned about instant replay demonstrating this fact.

The *assigning of blame* was also an important factor in the bottle riot. Browns fans thought the referee had made the wrong decision to institute an instant replay examination, because the quarterback had already snapped the ball on the next play, thus disallowing the possibility of instant replay in this particular case.

The *desire to punish* and *feelings of omnipotence* variables are more analytically useful when combined, because a desire to punish and feelings of omnipotence tend to work hand in hand. The fans clearly desired to punish the referee and other officials for conducting the instant replay and subsequently disallowing the original call. This desire was further exacerbated by the referee's decision to award the ball to the Jaguars after the Browns' loss of downs. Feelings of omnipotence are more difficult to measure, but it is clear that many fans thought they would not get in trouble by throwing bottles. Further, with forty-eight seconds to go, being thrown out of the game—which would have been the likely penalty—was not a factor in their decision.

Lastly, it should be noted that the instant replay evaluation took at least two minutes, thus allowing for a buildup of all the feelings previously noted. In summary, the data indicate that all five of the subdeterminants which facilitate the growth of a generalized belief were likely present among some members of the Browns fans in Cleveland. That is, feelings of anxiety, ambiguity, blame assignment, a desire to punish, and omnipotence influenced fans throughout the stadium. The question is, how widely shared were those beliefs? How generalized were they? Given the physical structure of the stadium where it is easy to see most fans and particularly those in the "Dawg Pound," it is safe to say that the beliefs about the referee's decision were widespread.

The eyewitnesses said that the bottle throwing came from all parts of the stadium, although one witness said he thought it began in the Dawg Pound.

Mobilization for Action

For the analysis of mobilization, I drew on personal interviews, newspaper accounts, and photographs about persons or events. In reference to persons, there does not seem to be any strong evidence that particular individuals were leaders, although the fact that the bottle throwing probably started in the Dawg Pound can be seen as a form of leadership. A Browns football crowd is fairly well organized before and during a game. This comes from physical symbols like Browns scarves, hats, and jackets, as well as items that make fun of the opposing team. In addition, most of the fans are season ticket holders and either know each other in the surrounding area or at least have some recognition of nearby fans. There is also a tradition of tailgating at the games, and, lastly, most people go to the game in groups ranging from two to eight people.

As has been stated, the configuration of the stadium plays a role because it is relatively easy to see fans in other sections, particularly the Dawg Pound. However, the distance from the fans to the field is quite long. Thus, many of the thrown bottles did not make it to the field but hit or came near to hitting other fans closer to the field. (This was also because the bottles were half full or empty and did not carry very well when thrown.)

The hostile outburst is divided into two basic phases that the Smelser model describes: the initial and derived phases. The initial phase began when the Cleveland Browns fans shouted obscenities and threw missiles at the referee and other officials. This was followed by an attempt by a small number of Browns fans to get to the field and the officials. Who were the fans who carried out the hostile outburst? Photographs and eyewitness reports indicate that most were white males under forty. The arrest records show that those who were arrested were males under thirty, although those arrested were not cited for bottle throwing.

The derived phase happened about a half hour later when the game resumed for one play and the bottle throwing began, although not with the intensity of the initial phase of the hostile outburst.

Social Control

For Smelser, social control is an important part of any collective behavior episode. It is not distinct and separate but is part of the value-added process at any stage. With regard to the Cleveland beer bottle riot, there was one major breakdown in this social process: the lack of social control by some Browns fans in the face of a perceived error by the referee leading to the negative impact on their team's playoff chances. If the analysis is correct that the generalized belief was widespread, the interesting question becomes not why were there so many people involved in the riot, but why were there so few? The answer seems to lie in the presence of internal social control agents.

It is likely that most Browns fans came with other people to the game. These people could have acted as cheerleaders; however, it is quite possible that they could have acted in the capacity of social control by encouraging their companions *not* to throw bottles. I would conjecture that the reason given for not throwing bottles was not out of a concern for the referee or other officials, but for fans who were below the bottle throwers and might get hit. One of my eyewitnesses, Hensley, was close to the field and was hit on the arm. Press reports stated that there were some injuries from bottle throwers.

A second aspect of social control was the distance involved. Because the sight lines are so good in the stadium, potential bottle throwers would likely realize that their missiles would not reach the officials, which was clearly the goal of the fans. Photographic evidence shows considerable bottle throwing near the exit where the referee and other officials left the field (*Plain Dealer* 2001 [December 17], A-1).

Lastly, the bottle throwers ran out of missiles. As it was late in the game, there were few full bottles left to throw at the officials. While half-full or empty bottles would work, they clearly would not travel as far as a full bottle.

There was also an external social control at the riot. This was in the form of police and other security staff who prevented fans from running on the field (*Akron Beacon Journal* 2001 [December 23], D-4).

Studying the Police

In concluding this chapter on researching fan violence, I want to discuss the topic of doing research on the social control forces. Social control refers to those responses at the individual and group levels that prevent and/or manage the fan violence in reference to winning or losing. While social control means more than policing, the activities of the police are a focus of this analysis. To illuminate the American experience, I am going to contrast it with my experiences working with the English police. There are many differences between American and English sporting events which need to be considered when looking for reasons for police actions.

First, American fan violence occurs in several sports—including baseball, football, basketball, hockey, and boxing—while in England it takes place almost exclusively at soccer matches. (There have been reports of violence at cricket matches, but this is quite rare.) Second, American violence happens at several levels of competition, while in England it occurs exclusively at professional soccer matches. Third, violence in the United States takes place more often during championship play, while in England it happens anytime during the season, from friendly (exhibition) matches on to the Football Association Championship.

All this leads to the fact that American police are much less experienced at handling unruly sports crowds than English police. English police have developed a variety of skills that allow them to fine-tune their responses to crowd actions and circumstances. For example, in the mid-1980s, after the Yorkshire miners' strike ended, a West Midlands policeman told me that he thought that one of the reasons why no miners died at the hands of the police was because the police had such a depth of experience, from soccer, in dealing with unruly crowds. The police, he thought, generalized these skills to other types of crowd actions.

In the United States, high-ranking police officers are more willing to talk about their crowd control activities and the reasons behind their decisions than are officers from the lower ranks. This may be partly due to the fact that crowd control is more interesting for the higher ranks than for the lower ones. By *interesting* I mean that, in a sense, controlling a crowd has elements of a chess match with moves and countermoves. The typical policeman in the United States is not privy to strategies and policies except in a narrow operational sense and, hence, is less interested in the entire process.

In contrast, English officers, at all levels, seem to have more input into the policing process of crowd control. In research on English soccer crowds, I conducted interviews with police constables from the highest to the lowest ranks. The police were generally quite candid with me about reasons for various decisions. For example, when an arrest or ejection from the ground was made, I asked reasons for action and the constables were, for the most part, willing to discuss their actions with me.

Interviews with police must be done as soon as possible after the crowd action as police have a tendency to put things behind rather quickly. No doubt, this forgetting pattern is good mental health, but it is tough on the researcher. Police are good at describing the actions of the individuals who were arrested but are seldom very introspective as why certain individuals were arrested while others doing the same thing were not. The sociologist should also interview other people who might have insights into social control, such as reporters, venders, and nonviolent fans.

In the United States the police structure is more diffused and less hierarchical than in England. Thus, permission to conduct interviews can be obtained at a lower command level. In contrast, in England, as well as other parts of the United Kingdom, permission must be obtained from the chief constable or his deputy. Also, in the United States the police are more informal in reference to rank. Seldom do you see salutes or "yes sir/no sir (or ma'am)" when lower ranks interact with higher ranks. In England, policing is done in a paramilitary structure. It is a disciplined force, and courtesies between ranks are expected and exercised. The researcher is expected to follow these courtesies and loss of rapport can happen if he or she becomes too informal.

Newspaper articles are not very helpful in describing the activities of the police in dealing with violent crowds. However, these accounts are a useful, if sometimes unreliable, source for arrest data. This characterization is true for both American and British newspapers. For reasons that are hard to fathom, police behavior is practically invisible to reporters. Unless something goes wrong, police are treated as "crowd referees." They are seen as essential, but always in the background. Indeed, social scientists have done more to bring typical police activity to the forefront than have journalists.

Seldom will a photographer take a picture of a policeman in action when violence breaks out, but the researcher should look at any such photos that are available. For example, several photographs, originally unpublished, of the Cleveland Browns beer bottle riot showed rather dramatically what policemen should not do in a riot—policemen were chasing fans around the outfield. These shots were obtained directly from the photographer as they were rejected by editors as unsuitable for the sports pages.

Photographs can also be used to study passive social control, such as signs, fences, and barriers. In both the United States and England, photographers generally take pictures from the field or pitch, shooting up into the crowd. This generally provides good data on the density of the crowd. It also provides, for English soccer crowds, insights into the structure of the terraces.

Summary

In this chapter I argued that an understanding of sports fan violence is possible when the investigator is not present when the riot happens. Using a protocol, I argued that research on fan violence needs to be theoretically grounded and, where possible, comparative. I have shown the linkage between the theoretical models presented in chapter 2 and various data sources. I hope that this protocol will also encourage and facilitate cross-cultural research on crowds in general and sports crowds in particular. In the next chapter, I illustrate the protocol with a celebrating riot that took place after the 2002 Ohio State–Michigan game.

Notes

1. The protocol section was originally published in Jerry M. Lewis, "A Protocol for the Comparative Analysis of Sports Crowd Violence," *International Journal of Mass Emergencies and Disasters*, 1988: 211–25. I wish to thank the International Sociological Association Research Committee on Disasters for permission to use this material.

2. They were Thomas R. Hensley, a professor of political science at Kent State University; Doug Johnson, a Cleveland sports television producer; and Damon M. Lewis, my son.

References

Akron Beacon Journal. 2001. December 18, 23, passim.

Canton Repository. 2001. December 17, passim.

Danzger, H. M. 1975. "Validating Conflict Data." *American Sociological Review* 40 (5): 570–84.

Earl, J., A. Martin, J. D. McCarthy, and S. A. Soule. 2004. "The Use of Newspaper Data in the Study of Collective Action." W. R. Scott (ed.). *Annual Review of Sociology* 30: 65–80.

Kent-Ravenna *Record-Courier*. 2001. December 17, passim.

Lewis, J. M. 1972. "A Study of the Kent State Incident Using Smelser's Theory of Collective Behavior." *Sociological Inquiry* 42 (2): 87–96.

———. 1989. "A Value-Added Analysis of the Heysel Stadium Soccer Riot." *Current Psychology* 8 (1): 15–29.

Plain Dealer. 2001. December 17, 21, passim.

Smelser, N. J. 1962. *Theory of Collective Behavior*. New York: The Free Press.

Smith, M. 1978. "Precipitants of Crowd Violence." *Sociological Inquiry*. 48 (2): 121–31.

Stahler J. 2001. Cartoon. *Cincinnati Post*. Reprinted in *USA Today*, February 21, 15A.

Webb, E. J., D. T. Campbell, R. D. Schwartz, and L. Sechrist. 1966. *Unobtrusive Measures: Nonreactive Research in the Social Sciences*. Chicago: Rand McNally.

4

Social Correlates of Sports Fan Violence

The Cleveland Baseball Beer Riot

Certain sports riots take on almost mythic qualities, and the Cleveland Indians beer riot is such an event. The Cleveland Indians hosted the Texas Rangers on a Tuesday evening, June 4, 1974, for a baseball game. It was "Beer Night," a promotion that allowed each fan to get six 10-cent cups of beer.

A week before the game there had been a fight in Texas between members of these two teams. The manager of the Texas team at the time was Billy Martin, a highly controversial figure. My students reported to me that the radio broadcaster for the Indians had said, "Come down to Beer Night and let's stick it in Billy Martin's ear."

Shortly before the game, Billy Martin was introduced to the fans and was greeted with a chorus of boos and catcalls. He reacted by tipping his hat and blowing kisses to fans.

This chapter is a revision of parts of Jerry M. Lewis, "Fan Violence: An American Social Problem," in *Research in Social Problems and Public Policy*, ed. M. Lewis, vol. 2, 175–206 (Greenwich, CT: JAI Press, 1982).

Interruptions by fans racing across the outfield began about the fourth inning and increased as the game wore on. At first, the running in the outfield occurred only between innings, but soon it was happening between outs and, finally, between pitches. In the sixth inning, one of the youths who raced across the outfield stopped and disrobed. He then streaked back and forth across the outfield (wearing only his socks) until he climbed over the right-field fence into the arms of a waiting policeman.

With two out in the ninth inning, some young fans attempted to shake the hand of the Rangers' right fielder. Then they tried to take his hat. When the Rangers dugout saw this, they thought the player needed help and raced out to right field with bats in hand. When the players in the Indians dugout saw the Ranger team rushing out, they, too, ran out to supply support for the Rangers. At the same time that both teams were rushing to the outfield, hundreds of fans in the right-field stands climbed over the railings and ran onto the field, and a confrontation between fans and players was under way.

The Indians and Rangers joined forces to protect themselves from the unruly mob. The brawl, fans versus players, went on for nearly ten minutes. It never totally stopped, but at least the Rangers and Indians were able to get away and head for their dugouts. However, by the time the Rangers got as far as the pitching mound, another brawl broke out, again with players fighting against fans.

Many of the players suffered bruises. The most serious injury was suffered by a Cleveland player who was hit on the head and shoulders with a steel folding chair that was tossed out of the stands.

At least eleven persons were arrested for disorderly conduct at the stadium and were taken to Central Police Station that night. Five of the people charged with rioting were fined $33.65 and ordered to the workhouse for three days. Also, a seventeen-year-old faced charges on juvenile delinquency.

For several days after the riot, newspapers investigated the situation to try to understand why the riot happened. When the riot started, Cleveland police sergeant Herbert J. Forray, who was on the stadium detail, called for outside help to strengthen his force, which consisted of one off-duty Cleveland police officer and fifty stadium police. Forray said that twenty cars from the tactical and impact units and the 3rd, 4th, and 5th districts responded.

Umpire Nestor Chylak said in a newspaper interview that he "saw trouble coming as early as the seventh inning and that the umpires began to plan for their safe exit. " (Lewis 1982, 185). Pictures show the umpires in a huddle talking over the situation arising between the fans and the Ranger team. Chylak also said in a *Plain Dealer* interview that he "saw two knives out there" and that the situation during the game was "like a zoo." (Lewis 1982, 185).

Billy Martin, manager of the Rangers, said he thought that Chylak should have called the game earlier, "when our bullpen had to come in." (Lewis 1982, 185). This was in the seventh inning, and several pictures show most of the Texas players sitting in their dugout with bats in their hands, just waiting for something to happen.

Many players on both teams said in newspaper interviews that the media were to blame for the riot, because there had been a fight between these same two teams a week earlier and many players thought the incident was blown out of proportion.

To understand this riot and others, this chapter examines factors sociologists call social correlates. That is, we are looking for variables that can be linked to fan violence and help us understand it. Sociologists use several sets of social correlates. Some—*structural variables*—are more general and abstract than others, and they look at the larger society and its relationships to fan violence. In contrast, *demographic variables* are less general and abstract and look at specific factors and their connections to fan violence. Structural variables are patterned social relationships that form the foundation for society, while demographic variables refer to characteristics of persons. The next section of this chapter discusses structural variables associated with fan violence, followed by an analysis of demographic factors. In a few places I will draw on British soccer hooliganism sources in the absence of North American data.

Structural Variables and Sports Fan Violence

This section on structural variables begins with a case history of the Michigan State basketball riot.

It was Saturday evening March 27, 1999. Michigan State had just lost a Final Four game in the Division I basketball tournament. Estimates put the crowd size at five thousand to ten thousand and the amount of property damage at over $250,000 (Eder 2003). The riot was near the Michigan State campus in the streets and in an off-campus housing complex. The riot began about 10:08 p.m., before the game had finished, with bottles being thrown at police. The initial teargassing of students and others began about 11:23 p.m. Quiet was restored early Sunday morning. The rioting activities included chanting and gesturing; vandalism; and the setting of fire to couches, trees, and cars, including police cars. The crowd events generated a total of 132 arrests eventually resulting in 55 sentenced felonies and 58 misdemeanors (Eder 2003). Seventy-one of those arrested were Michigan State students. Thus, over half of those arrested were college students.

The major structural variables that scholars of sports fan violence should consider are the type of sport, competition importance, perceived officiating errors, racial and ethnic tensions. These variables are considered structural because they are part of the organization of sport. I will review each structural variable and then present and analyze newspaper data to evaluate the relative importance of each for explaining fan violence.

The Structural Variables

Sport Types

North America has developed the most pluralistic sports culture known to the human experience. It becomes necessary to look at both the sport type and level of competition. Two questions about fan violence are often raised: Are some sports more likely to have fan violence than others? Do professional sports generate more fan violence than collegiate sports? The analyst should deal with these questions by looking at the structural characteristics associated with the distribution of fan violence by sport and level of competition in North America.

Importance of the Competition

There are three situations that should be studied when looking at the importance of the competition: entries into championship play, championship play itself, and traditional rivalries. The first factor is access to the championship series. This refers to competitions that are typically referred to as playoffs or season-ending series that lead to playoffs or championships. The second factor is the actual championship itself. All sports have a season-ending championship, and this becomes, de facto, *the* most important game of the season for fans of both teams.

The third factor is traditional rivalries between opponents who have a history of competition that is deemed by fans and the media as an important game to win, or not to lose. For example, in collegiate football, the Ohio State–Michigan game is seen by some as the most important traditional rivalry. Others would note the Army-Navy game. In professional baseball, an important rivalry is the New York Yankees–Boston Red Sox competition. A major riot took place at the Ohio State–Michigan football game in 2002 and is analyzed in chapter 6, along with the Red Sox riot.

Perceived Officiating Errors

Officiating errors are often suggested as a cause of fan violence. Fans of the losing team frequently give this reason for sports riots. It should be noted that the officiating error is often a perceived error and not an actual one, as instant replays often show fans.

Racial and Ethnic Tensions

Many riots in American history are associated with racial or ethnic tensions. For example, the Rodney King riots in Los

Angeles in April of 1992 involved Blacks, Latinos, Koreans, and Whites (Baldassare 1994). The sports sociologist should attempt to determine if sports riots have any linkages to racial and/or ethnic tensions.

In addition to the structural variables, there are two questions regarding the statistics of fan violence that should be considered by researchers:

1. When did sports fan violence begin in North America?
2. Is sports fan violence increasing or decreasing in North America?

Gathering the Data

These are not easy questions to answer, particularly in the absence of a national data-gathering source such as the *London Times* in Britain. Neither the United States nor Canada has a single newspaper that covers the entire country. Consequently, a search program was necessary to generate a body of information that could address these questions and others in relation to structural variables.

When I began my research on sports fan violence in the mid-1970s, I undertook a systematic effort to discover answers to the structural factors as well as the questions that I just posed. Through the help of several classes of collective behavior students, I conducted a content analysis looking for stories on sports riots of any type. The design called for searching the front page of the paper and the front page of the sports section for reports of sports fan violence. The years were 1960 to 1972, with papers used being those available for this time period in full runs in the Kent State University library. Students received academic credit for their efforts. The data were based on seven major East Coast and Midwest newspapers: the *Akron Beacon Journal*, *Atlanta Journal-Constitution*, *Boston Globe*, Cleveland *Plain Dealer*, *New York Times*, *St. Louis Post-Dispatch*, and *Washington Post*. Since only the *New York Times* had an index, the first page of the sports section was searched for reports of fan violence.

Because the searching of newspaper archives was so labor intensive and of questionable academic value to my students, I tried a different approach for collecting data from 1973 to 1984. An index was obtained for each of the following newspapers: the *Chicago Tribune,* Cleveland *Plain Dealer, Los Angeles Times,* New Orleans *Times-Picayune, New York Times,* and *Washington Post.* The indices were searched for newspaper articles related to fan violence, generating a result of N = 34 riots. This is much lower than the number of riots for 1960 to 1972 (N = 171). It may be that this searching procedure is not as sensitive to identifying riots as is the technique of reading the papers directly as in the initial search process. As I identified fan violence through indices, my research assistants coded the riots using the same procedures as for the years 1960 to 1972.

The third wave of data collection was for the years 1985 to 2004 using LexisNexis, a newspaper archive that has become and will continue to be an important source of data for collective behavior scholars. Recently, sociologists Kaplowitz and Campo (2004) and Clark McPhail and his associates (McCarthy, Martin, and McPhail 2005) have used LexisNexis to locate newspaper stories on fan violence. Kaplowitz and Campo found, beginning in 1995, a total of 24 sports-related riots on 15 campuses. McCarthy and colleagues noted two basic types of crowd actions associated with college campuses—protest and convivial gatherings, with convivial gatherings, including sports riots, being much larger than protest gatherings.

I used the LexisNexis search system to generate data by searching for key words found in papers throughout North America. The search for newspaper reports was for the years 1985 to 2004 using the key words and phrases *fan violence, sports fan violence, crowd violence, sports violence,* and *spectator violence. Fan violence* generated the most hits related to this research, but *sports violence* generated many hits as well, though the hits were not germane to my research on crowd fan violence. For example, player fights were hits for *sports violence,* but these were not appropriate stories to include in the research. Regional categories were searched first, that is, *Midwest Regional Sources* and then the

Table 4.1. Fan Violence Newspaper Reports for Football, Baseball, Basketball, and Hockey, by Level and Importance of Competition, 1960–1972

	Football N = 43	Baseball N = 36	Basketball N = 35	Hockey N = 15
1. *Level of Competition*				
a. High School	37.2%	2.8%	34.3%	—
b. College	23.3%	8.3%	45.7%	—
c. Professional	37.2%	88.9%	17.1%	100%
d. Other	2.3%	—	2.9%	—
2. *Importance of Competition*				
a. Nonchampionship	53.5%	63.9%	68.6%	93.3%
b. Championship	46.5%	36.1%	31.4%	6.7%

state, for example, *Illinois*. Reports of riots were counted once even though some appeared several times. For example, the Ohio State–Michigan Football riot in 2002 (discussed in chapter 6) was a "hit" in many papers, but only counted once for this research. I did the coding for the years 1985 to 2004. The three sets of data are reported in tables 4.1 to 4.3.

Table 4.2. Fan Violence Newspaper Reports for Football, Baseball, Basketball, and Hockey by Level and Importance of Competition, 1973–1984

	Football N = 9	Baseball N = 7	Basketball N = 8	Hockey N = 1
1. *Level of Competition*				
a. High School	11.1%	—	62.5%	—
b. College	22.2%	—	37.5%	—
c. Professional	66.7%	100%	—	100%
2. *Importance of Competition*				
a. Nonchampionship	66.7%	57.1%	100%	100%
b. Championship	33.3%	42.9%	—	—

Table 4.3. Fan Violence Newspaper Reports at Football, Baseball, Basketball, and Hockey by Level and Importance of Competition, 1985–2004

	Football N = 27	Baseball N = 7	Basketball N = 14	Hockey N = 8
1. Level of Competition				
a. High School	7.4%	14.2%	—	12.5%
b. College	48.2%	—	42.8%	25%
c. Professional	44.4%	85.8%	57.2%	62.5%
2. Importance of Competition				
a. Nonchampionship	74%	28.4%	28.5%	25%
b. Championship	26%	71.6%	71.5%	75%

Results of the Newspaper Analysis

To review: Fan violence is defined as collective violence involving five or more spectators, in coordination, before, during, or after a formally organized sporting event attended by at least one hundred people. With regard to our newspaper data, the actual forms of fan violence included throwing missiles; vandalism; running onto the playing field or court, thus disrupting the event; arson; and fighting between fans, fans and players, and fans and social control agents. Each of these was considered a sufficient condition of fan violence, but the forms often occurred in combination.

1960–1972

The sample of newspapers for 1960–1972 showed that in regard to sport type, 75 percent (129 out of 171) of the fan violence incidents (involving five or more fans) took place in four major team sports. They were football, baseball, basketball, and hockey. Three sports—football, baseball, and basketball—accounted for 67 percent of the cases of fan violence. Most of the violence takes place at the collegiate and professional levels of competition. However, about 30 percent of the violence in football and basketball occurs at the high school level.

The importance of the competition is a factor in fan violence associated with football and baseball. However, it was less of a factor in basketball and hockey. The traditional rivalry does not seem to be an important factor for any of the episodes of fan violence. Thus, "we lost the game, but won the fight afterward" is an unwarranted stereotype about fan violence.

Officiating errors, a factor often mentioned in major soccer riots, does not seem to be a factor for football, baseball, or basketball, but is a factor for boxing and hockey.

In regard to sites, most fan violence takes place at one location which is on, or near, the playing area.

The data were coded for four social problems: racial conflict, economic problems, strikes, and school-related problems. Only racial conflict was discovered as a factor, and was very limited at that. Racial conflict was seen as a cause in 15 percent of the incidents of spectator violence involving football and 16 percent involving basketball. The concentration of racial conflict was primarily in high schools.

1973–1984

The results for 1973–1984 show both similarities and differences to the data from 1960 to 1972. As shown in table 4.3, the similarities were that 74 percent of the riots came from four sports—football, baseball and basketball and hockey—with 71 percent from the first three sports. In addition, officiating errors, traditional rivalries, and social problems were not factors in the riots. The riots were generally at one site.

A major difference in the two sets of data, beyond the sample size, is in the championship/nonchampionship category, specifically with regard to football, baseball, and basketball. In the later set, only 21 percent of the riots were associated with championships, in contrast with 38 percent in the earlier data.

1985–2004

The results for 1985–2004 follow a pattern similar to the early research. Four sports—football, baseball, basketball, and hockey—generated fifty-six out of the fifty-seven incidents of crowd violence. The fifty-seventh riot was after a women's Final Four game and was not counted. Three sports—football, baseball, and basketball—accounted for 84 percent of the riots. Forty-nine percent of the riots involved championship play.

The overall pattern of the data from newspaper reports for the years 1960–2004 show that there were 256 riots meeting the definition of a sports riot. Two hundred nine of these are presented in tables 4.1 to 4.3. The data do not support Smelser's strain theory presented in chapter 2. Rather, the violence seems to follow Marx's (1970) notion of being issueless. This conclusion is warranted by (1) the limited number of reports of social problems (strain) associated with the violence; (2) the concentration of the fan violence in the college and professional levels; and (3) the location of the violence at one site generally on, or near, the stadium of the winning team in an easily accessible urban area. While Smelser's strain model seems to hold for some studies of student unrest (Lewis 1972), it does not apply to spectator violence. It may be that within structural conduciveness it is possible to see one type of violence based on strain and another based on characteristics of the situation (issueless).

The violence, as reflected in these reports, seems to be tied directly to the sport per se. This is particularly true for football and baseball, which account for 50 percent of the cases of fan violence, with very little mention of social problems in the newspaper stories. Championship play, which accounted for a small proportion of games played, has been increasing as a source of violence: 35 percent for the years 1960–1972 but 50 percent for 1985–2004.

These newspaper reports show how United States fan violence differs from European, particularly British, fan violence. The 256 incidents of fan violence, with 210 representing the top four team sports in attendance (tables 4.1 to 4.3), differ in several ways. First, there are more sports involved. British fan violence is associated mainly with soccer (football) to such an extent that in Britain, violent fans have an identity and are known as "soccer hooligans." Second, the fact that North America has fan violence at the collegiate and high school levels of competition shows a sharp contrast with Britain, where almost all of the violence is associated with professional competition. Third, United States fan violence has not reached the level of seriousness seen with British fan violence, as exemplified in the riots at Heysel (Lewis 1989; appendix C) and Hillsborough (Lewis and Kelsey 1994).

Demographic Characteristics of Violent Sports Fans

This analysis will look at each of these demographic variables as they relate to sports fan violence at both the collegiate and professional levels of sport. It contrasts North American fan violence with the violence that happens in Europe, particularly Britain. The analysis begins with collegiate sports fan violence and follows with professional sports fan violence. For all the evidence, I report the earliest to the most recent. The chapter concludes with a discussion of why certain categories of individuals tend to get involved more often than others get involved. Here I examine six demographic characteristics, including gender, age, race, occupation, income, and religion, and the possible linkage of these variables to fan violence. Although gender and age are closely tied in understanding fan violence, I begin with the most important demographic variable related to fan violence: gender. This is because previous research, in both North America and Europe, has shown that the most important variable in understanding sports fan violence is gender.

This review of the literature has been greatly aided by two earlier reviews. Kevin Young (2002, 240–47) examined the literature, in a multicultural context, on what violent fans do. The five behavior categories included missile throwing, using weapons and firearms, field invasions, vandalism, and fans fighting each other. In my experience, based on field work and interviews, fan violence in the United States involves primarily missile throwing and vandalism.

The other review was published by Gordon Russell (2004), who looked at the social-psychological characteristics of people involved in sports riots. His analysis was multicultural as well.

Russell's review (2004, passim) concluded that in terms of demographic factors, violent fans tended to be males who had strong identification with a team, athlete, or country.

Gender and Collegiate Sports Violence

Gender and age have long been seen as the major correlates of riot participation (McPhail 1971). Beginning with gender and following with age, I will look first at collegiate fan violence and then professional sports riot violence. Most of the collegiate fan violence is located in men's sports, particularly first division football, basketball, and hockey.

To provide insight into gender, college students, and fan violence, I start with the results of an experiment I conducted on the perception of fan violence by college students. I asked students in a large university located in Northeast Ohio to evaluate news stories about fan violence. The Football/Hockey Riot Study design is a factorial expansion of the Post-test Only Control Group design in its simplest form (Campbell and Stanley 1963). The Post-test Only Control Group design consists of exposing two groups of students to the experimental variable, which in this case was the type of sport (football versus hockey) and the level of violence severity, then measuring both the experimental group and the control group. *Post-test* means that there is no before measure, only an after measure.

This design may be expanded by adding to the number of experimental variables and the number of groups, with or without a control group. These experimental treatments may be divided into different treatment levels. In the Football/Hockey Riot Study, students were randomly assigned to two groups through the randomization of two experimental questionnaire forms. Both groups underwent experimental treatment. To facilitate the administration of the questionnaires, both forms were given to two separate beginning sociology classes at different times on the same day.

Each student was randomly given a questionnaire containing five vignettes reportedly taken from newspaper stories on football riots or hockey riots. They were actually based on Wanderer's

(1969) Index of Riot Severity and ranged in severity from a low level to a high level. The stories on the football riot and hockey riot forms were identical, with the only difference being that the words *football* and *hockey* were interchanged.

The vignettes were placed on the questionnaire in a random order, with the placement identical for both questionnaires. After the respondents read each story, they were asked to answer eight questions before going to the next story. Finally, they were asked to answer some demographic questions. For control purposes, two additional sets of questionnaires using the phrases *environmental protest* or *rock concert* were also handed out. These data are not reported here. The students were debriefed after turning in the questionnaires.

Figure 4.1 presents the stories for low and high levels of severity. The first wave of data was gathered in 1979 and published in 1982 (Lewis 1982). In 2004, I replicated this study. The results for 1982 are reported in table 4.4 and the results for 2004 are covered in table 4.5.

Low Severity

> *Football:* Last night a crowd of football fans vented their enthusiasm after a game by breaking store windows. Damage was estimated at $5,000.
> *Hockey:* Last night a crowd of hockey fans vented their enthusiasm after a game by breaking store windows. Damage was estimated at $5,000.

High Severity

> *Football:* City and state police and the National Guard were mobilized last night as football fans became destructive. Looting, fire, and vandalism went unchecked for hours as the authorities battled the crowd in an attempt to eliminate gunfire and restore order. Damage was estimated in the hundreds of thousands of dollars. Two people were killed (a fan and a police officer). Numerous injuries were also reported.
> *Hockey:* City and state police and the National Guard were mobilized last night as hockey fans became destructive. Looting, fire, and vandalism went unchecked for hours as the authorities battled the crowd in an attempt to eliminate gunfire and restore order. Damage was estimated in the hundreds of thousands of dollars. Two people were killed (a fan and a police officer). Numerous injuries were also reported.

Figure 4.1.   The Vignettes Used in the Perception Study

Table 4.4. Attitudes of Males and Females, by Violence Severity and Sport, toward Spectator Violence (1982)

	Football/Hc		male	Female
	Male (N = 91)		108)	Female (N = 108)
Category	Low Seve	›ity	High Severity
Approve of friends' partic			
Yes	2%		—
Probably	5%		2%
Probably not	25%		8%
No	63%		9%
Self-Participation?			
Yes	2%	4	—
Probably	2%	1%	1%
Probably not	20%	15%	9%	4%
No	76%	80%	91.1%	95%

(handwritten note: "Females Don't like riding")

Table 4.5. Attitudes of Males and Females, by Violence Severity and Sport, toward Spectator Violence (2004)

	Football/Hockey			
	Male (N = 58)	Male (N = 58)	Female (N = 126)	Female (N = 126)
Category	Low Severity	High Severity	Low Severity	High Severity
Approve of friends' participation?				
Yes	5%	5%	1%	1%
Probably	26%	12%	5%	3%
Probably not	31%	31%	31%	13%
No	38%	62%	64%	83%
Self-Participation?				
Yes	34%	3%	21%	3%
Probably	33%	10%	33%	3%
Probably not	26%	21%	29%	9%
No	7%	66%	17%	85%

In approaching these two sets of data, separated by twenty-five years, I want to highlight similarities and differences between men and women for the years 1982 and 2004. For this analysis (see tables 4.4 and 4.5) I combined football and hockey results since there is no significant differences by sport in the data sets.

It should be noted that the vignettes do not indicate whether the violence is collegiate or professional sports. The results show that it is mostly males who would be willing to get involved in high-severity fan violence at a football or hockey match. Ralph Turner (1969) has suggested that crowd violence is often interpreted in terms of folk concepts. Following this idea, it seems to be clear to many that low-level violence and gender are, and "should be," connected. The folk concept is that low levels of fan violence are approved behavior for male sports fans. These data suggest that the folk concept of fan violence as being "boys will be boys" is the "correct" perception of the situation by many college students.

In both years (not in the tables) men and women students described the low-severity riot as smaller than the high-severity crowds as measured by estimated crowd size. However, in the 2004 data for high severity in the category 501+ (estimated crowd size) the responses changed. Fifty-two percent of the males in 1982 placed the high-severity crowd in this category, while this was true for 26 percent in 2004. The data suggest that severity of rioting was perceived as happening in smaller crowds by 2004. Perhaps males think that smaller crowds can be as violent as larger crowds. Female students follow a similar pattern with 31 percent in 1982 compared to 13 percent in 2004 putting the high-severity crowd at over five hundred people.

The Approval of Fan Violence

The analysis now turns to the most important data on attitudes—that is, the willingness of college students to approve of their friends as well as their own participation in a celebrating sports riot. Looking only at the high-severity vignette (figure 4.1), the 1982 data (table 4.4), using the "yes" and "probably" re-

sponses, show that 6 percent of the males and 2 percent of the females approve of their friends' participation in a high-severity
riot. In 2004 these figures were 17 percent and 4 percent, respectively—a tripling for men and doubling for women. Of course,
the good news is that most students reported disapproval of their
friends' participating in a high-severity riot, with 83 percent of
women and 62 percent of men saying "no" to approval. Women
should be seen as a resource for discouraging men from participating in fan violence. I will say more about this in chapter 8.

In regard to self-participation in high-severity riots, the results are cause for concern. In 1982 5 percent of males and 2 percent of females were willing to participate in a football or hockey
sports riot vignette where two people died. Those numbers increased in 2004, with 13 percent of males and 6 percent of females indicating a willingness to participate in a high-severity
riot. Using the findings, is it possible to estimate the critical mass
of potential high-severity rioters? Let us assume that 40 percent
of those at an Ohio State–Michigan game with eighty thousand
in attendance are between eighteen and twenty-five years old
(thirty-two thousand individuals), with 60 percent male (nineteen thousand) and 40 percent female (thirteen thousand). Using
the 13 and 6 percent, respectively, of people approving high-
severity fan violence, about thirty-two hundred individuals
would be providing a critical mass of students and like-minded
people willing to participate in a riot where deaths have occurred. The policy implications of these findings are discussed in
chapter 8. A more detailed statistical analysis of the 2004 findings may be found in Kalkhoff and Lewis (2006).

Additional Gender Data

There are other kinds of empirical data that allow us to understand sports fan violence from a gender perspective. These
take the form of social science and newspaper data. I begin with
social science studies, citing the earliest material first. In an experimental study of young males (N = 78), with race not indicated, Russell and Arms (1998) found that the likelihood of
males joining in fan violence was linked to how recently they

had been in a fight and whether or not they enjoyed hockey player fights. Gender also influences the perception of fan violence. In their study of the 1999 Michigan State riot, Kaplowitz and Campo (2004) found in a survey of Michigan State students ($N = 2,008$) that men were more likely to condone and enjoy the riot than were women.

In December of 2002, following the Ohio State–Michigan riot (see chapter 6), I collected information from students in an Introduction to Sociology class. The students were mostly white with a mean age of 19.3. Nine days after the Ohio State incident I asked them this question: "Why do you think the football fans rioted at Ohio State after the Michigan Game?" Although students often gave several reasons, I coded only the first reason they provided. Here are the results by gender (Females = 157; Males = 83). Two reasons accounted for slightly over half of the answers: Thirty-one percent of the women attributed the riot to emotions such as excitement and happiness, while this was true of only 18 percent of the men. Twenty-five percent of both men and women mentioned drinking as the other factor.

Newspaper data can also be used to provide insights into fan violence and gender. The *Lansing (Michigan) State Journal* published several pictures of rioters in the 1999 Michigan State riot in its issues from March 29, 30, and 31, 1999. It is possible to identify sixty-three individuals in eight pictures at the riot scenes. Fifty-seven of these individuals are young, white males and six are young, white females. One dramatic photograph (*Lansing State Journal* 1999 [March 29], 5A) shows ten young, white males, working in coordination, attempting to turn over an already damaged police car.

In studying the Ohio State riot (see chapter 6), I was able to develop two sets of evidence that suggest that the rioters were primarily young, white males. First, using the *Columbus Dispatch* (2002) arrest data ($N = 57$), I determined that forty-eight of those arrested had male names, seven had female names, and two had names that could have been male or female. Of the forty males, the mean age was 22.6 years, with the range from 17–40. Thus, it can be concluded that of those arrested, the typical rioter was a young male. (While race cannot be determined very well from names, an inspection of the names suggests that those arrested were not African American or Asian.) Next, my assistant and I looked at photographs of the rioters at both the attack on the goal posts and the burning of cars on 13th Street. We examined the photographs independently and concluded that most of the individuals in the photographs were young, white males carrying out the action of the riot, that is, attacking the goalposts or burning cars.

Gender and Professional Sports Riots

Continuing the discussion of gender and violence, the analysis now turns to professional sports and fan violence. I found a similar pattern to collegiate fan violence. This analysis begins with a description of the Pittsburgh Super Bowl riot.

The Super Bowl win on January 13, 1975, was the first title a Steelers team had won in forty-two years. Gas stations, department stores, and many other businesses had "Go Steelers" signs posted, indicating that many in the town were ready to party should the Steelers win the game. Pittsburgh's morning paper, *The Press*, put "Go Steelers" on top of page 1, a further indication that many people in Pittsburgh were intensely interested in the game.

At one downtown hotel, the Hilton, more than one hundred rooms were converted into private areas and party centers. People arrived before the game with food, booze, and drugs to watch the game on television, since it was being played in New Orleans. In the halls of the Hilton, one could hear an enthusiastic response every time a call was favorable for the Steelers.

After the Steelers won the game, people started moving toward Market Square, an area dotted with nightclubs and after-hours places. Elevators at the hotel were jammed with drunken people. Many ignored police warnings to stay away until the next day to celebrate, and they roamed around in cold, wet snow, braving twenty-degree weather. Downtown streets were cluttered with parked cars even though there was a parking ban in effect.

Within a half hour after the end of the game, the crowd had grown to between ten and fifteen thousand. The majority of the people who gathered at Market Square to celebrate were young. The police permitted drinking and dope smoking. Four hundred extra police were added to the detail just in case things should get out of hand.

Police strategy was to stop matters early, because they didn't want the crowd to swell to extremely large numbers. They began to force the people apart, pushing them down streets in an effort to break up the mob. As police began to force people apart, the character of a portion of the crowd changed from that of a carefree, celebrating mass to an unruly, nasty aggregate of people.

Full beer bottles and cans were thrown from the crowd and from some downtown buildings. Downtown store windows were destroyed and police started to use billy clubs on some of the fans. Four police dogs were used at some of the trouble spots, and at one point, a dog was turned loose in the crowd and a rumor spread that someone's finger was bitten off. At least two back windows in police cars were broken and someone turned on a fire hydrant.

At one point, a police officer tried to arrest a young man and was subsequently pelted by beer bottles and snowballs by an angry mob that crowded to within two feet of him. One policeman was hit in the face with a full can of beer and suffered a fractured skull.

At 9:30 p.m. the police made an announcement over a bullhorn that anyone on the streets after ten o'clock in the evening would be arrested. A police sergeant later said in a newspaper interview that the police would usually not have been that drastic, but apparently their strategy worked, and their "show of force" did convince the people that they were serious. The streets were clear by 11:30 p.m. Press reports said that during the crowd actions, 224 people were arrested. However, no source was ever provided for that figure. The next night, after a welcoming home celebration and parade, more violence occurred in the same area, and more arrests were made.

In table 4.6 I compare individuals arrested during the Super Bowl riots with those arrested during antiwar protests in Chicago in 1968 and people arrested during racially oriented protests in various cities in the United States in 1967. The data in table 4.6 indicate that those who celebrated the Super Bowl victory were more likely to be white, male, and younger than their counterparts who were involved in episodes of violence related to antiwar or civil rights protests.

Table 4.6. Characteristics of Individuals Arrested at the 1975 Pittsburgh Super Bowl Celebration, the 1968 Chicago Anti-War Protest, and the 1967 Civil Disorders

| | Pittsburgh Arrests | | Chicago Arrests[a] | Civil Disorder Arrests[b] |
	January 12, 1975	January 13, 1975	1968	1967
	N = 101	N = 72	N = 668	
Sex				
Male	95%	94%	88%	89%
Female	4%	6%	12%	11%
Unknown	1%	—	—	—
				N = 11,415 (21 cities)
Age				
17 and under	19%	10%	10%	
18–20	15%	17%	33%	53%
21–25	51%	61%	33%	(15-24)
26 and over	14%	12%	23%	47%
Unknown	1%	—	1%	(25 +)
				N = 10,771 (16 cities)
Race				
White	91%	88%	c	15%
Black	2%	10%	c	83%
Other	—	—	c	1%
Unknown	7%	2%	c	1%
				N = 13,012 (22 cities)

NOTE:
[a]The data are from D. Walker, *Rights in Conflict* (New York: Bantam Books, 1968), 356–57.
[b]The data are from the *Report of the National Advisory Commission on Civil Disorders* (The Kerner Report; Washington, DC: U.S. Government Printing Office, 1968), passim.
[c]Racial data not reported.

Additional social science literature supports the conclusion that it is primarily males who get involved in fan violence. As table 4.6 shows, only 5 percent of the people arrested at the Pittsburgh Super Bowl riot were women. In England one study (Harrington 1968) found only one woman in its sample of 497 convicted football hooligans. A later study (Sports Council 1978) of Manchester United matches in England during the 1975–1976 season found no women ejected from or arrested at matches.

Journalistic accounts rarely report the gender of individuals involved in crowds. Newspaper and magazine accounts tend to describe the size of the crowd or the total numbers arrested. They usually refer to categories of people in terms such as fans, spectators, or hooligans. However, one case history did provide information on gender. The *Montreal Star*, in its study of the 1955 "Richard" riot, involving fans of the famous Canadian player, listed the names of thirty-one of the forty-one people arrested in the riot. All had masculine names except for the one person who gave only initials.

In regard to the Cleveland Browns beer bottle riot described in chapter 3, photographic evidence also indicates that the primary offenders at sporting matches are males. A colleague and I independently examined eleven published photographs of the Cleveland Browns beer bottle riot. All persons in the Cleveland Browns beer bottle riot pictures were judged by us as being white males. The discussion of the demographic variables moves from the issues of gender to other factors, beginning with age.

Age

The age variable is linked to the gender variable. The general impression, particularly from photographs, is that most people who participate in fan violence are under twenty-five. Assuming the traditional classification of college and university students is ages eighteen to twenty-four, this makes sense. In the previously discussed study, Russell and Arms (1998) found an inverse relationship between age and willingness to join fan violence.

In an examination of photographs of the 2002 Ohio State riot presented in chapter 6, my assistant and I found that in the published pictures of the rioting, most of the participants were young, white males. As already stated, of the forty-eight males arrested in the Ohio State riot, the mean age was 22.6 years with the range being 17–40.

Turning to the demographic characteristics of fans who get involved in professional sports fan violence, the pattern for the age of rioters is also clear. The social science literature suggests that individuals involved in professional sports fan violence are quite young. Those arrested at the 1975 Super Bowl riot were primarily under twenty-five. In England, the Harrington report (1968) indicates that the modal age category for convicted offenders was fifteen through nineteen. The Sports Council (1978) found that the average age for those arrested at Manchester United matches during the 1975–1976 season was nineteen years of age.

The *Montreal Star*'s report of the "Richard" riot listed the ages of those individuals who pled guilty on charges of disturbing the peace or obstructing traffic. The range was eighteen to thirty-five, with the mean being twenty-three years. Photographic evidence also indicates that those involved in fan violence are young. The Cleveland Browns beer bottle riot pictures supports the conclusion that most violent fans are relatively young.

Race

This is the factor that most researchers agree on. Race is not an important variable in fan violence in North America. It is clear from a variety of evidence, particularly photographs, that the typical person who gets involved in fan violence is going to be white. Blacks seldom get involved in sports fan violence of any kind, particularly celebrating violence. This is also true of Hispanics and Asians. This does not mean that Blacks, Hispanics, or Asians do not riot. They do, but the rioting tends to be political, as with the protests after the Rodney King verdict shows. According to Petersilia and Abrahamse (1994) in the Rodney King riots (April 30, to May 5, 1992), about 36 percent of those arrested were black and 51 percent Hispanic. In contrast virtually all of those arrested in the Pittsburgh Super Bowl riot were white.

Occupation and Income

There are no social science or newspaper studies on the relationship between fan violence and occupation for North America. While there is no solid information on this question, it is possible to speculate on what it might be by drawing on English soccer hooliganism data. In England, the Harrington report (1968), as well as the Sports Council (1978), indicate that the majority of people convicted for fan violence were unskilled or semiskilled workers. Seventy-six percent of those convicted for fan violence held semiskilled or unskilled jobs according to the Harrington report.

A 1996 report by Marsh and colleagues, *Football Violence in Europe*, notes that it is primarily the work of E. Dunning and his colleagues at Leicester University (Dunning 1994) that argues that soccer hooliganism in Britain is a working class phenomenon.

Education

No social science study reported the amount of education by those involved in fan violence. However, data from England are suggestive. Both the Harrington report (1968) and the Sports Council report (1978) indicated that from 16 to 21 percent of those convicted of fan violence in England were in school. Again, I found no journalistic or pictorial evidence that would contribute to our knowledge about education and fan violence.

Religion

I could find only one North American study that dealt with the relationship of religion and fan violence. Katz (1955, 108) found that most of the "Richard" rioters were Roman Catholic but no indication was made as to the role of religion in the riot. It should be noted that religious conflict is mentioned as a factor in Glasgow, Scotland, and Liverpool, England, football matches. For example, it was suggested to me by members of the Birmingham, England, police that sectarian tensions were factors in fan violence associated with Scotland's Rangers and Celtics and England's Liverpool and Everton football clubs.

It has been noted that religious conflict might be linked to fan violence in some urban high school football games in the United States, but that indication has never been documented with social science or newspaper data. There has never been a suggestion that North American fan violence is linked to religious variables at the collegiate level. This variable is by far the most under-researched dimension of demographic variables related to fan violence. Why is this the case? First, it may be that sectarian issues are simply not influential variables in fan violence. Second, it may be that it is too difficult to measure religion and link it to fan violence. Third, since religion is so pervasive and important in the United States, it may be seen as too sensitive an issue to raise vis-à-vis its linkage to sports fan violence.

Summary

For North America, and particularly the United States, the data on fan violence at the collegiate and professional levels of competition are clear. The typical rioter is likely to be a young, white male celebrating a victory after a championship or an important game or match. This question should be asked: Are young, white males socialized into becoming violent fans? An approach to answering this question is presented in the next chapter.

References

Baldassare, M., ed. 1994. *The Los Angeles Riots: Lessons for the Urban Future*. Boulder, CO: Westview Press.

Campbell, D. T., and J. C. Stanley. 1963. *Experimental and Quasi-Experiments Designs for Research*. Chicago: Rand McNally.

Columbus Dispatch. 2002. November 22, passim.

Dunning, E. 1994. "The Social Roots of Soccer Hooliganism: A Reply to the Critics of the 'Leicester School.'" In *Football and Social Identity*, ed. R. Giulianotti, N. Bonny, and M. Hepworth, 128–58. London: Routledge.

Eder, S. 2003. "City Hopes Hard-Line Sentencing Curbs Riots." *State News*, September 30. www.statenews.com.

Harrington, J. A. 1968. *Soccer Hooliganism: A Preliminary Report to Mr. Denis Howell, Minister of Sport*. Bristol: John Wright and Sons.

Kalkhoff, W., and J. M. Lewis. 2006. "College Student Perceptions of Sports Fan Violence." Unpublished manuscript, Kent State University, Kent, OH.

Kaplowitz, S. A., and S. Campo. 2004. "Drinking, Alcohol Policy, and Attitudes toward a Campus Riot." *Journal of College Student Development* 45, no. 5 (September/October): 1–10.

Katz, S. 1955. "Richard Hockey Riot." *Maclean's Magazine* (September 17): 11–15, 97–108.

Lansing State Journal. 1999. March 29, 30, 31, passim.

Lewis, J. M. 1972. "A Study of the Kent State Incident Using Smelser's Theory of Collective Behavior." *Sociological Inquiry* 42 (2): 87–96.

———. 1982. "Fan Violence: An American Social Problem." In *Research in Social Problems and Public Policy*, ed. M. Lewis, vol. 2, 175–206. Greenwich, CT: JAI Press.

———. 1989. "A Value-Added Analysis of the Heysel Stadium Soccer Riot." *Current Psychology* 8 (1): 15–29.

Lewis, J. M., and M. L. Kelsey. 1994. "The Crowd Crush at Hillsborough: The Collective Behavior of an Entertainment Crush." In *Disasters, Collective Behavior, and Social Organization*, ed. R. R. Dynes and K. J. Tierney, 190–206. Newark: University of Delaware Press.

Marsh, P., K. Fox, G. Carnibella, J. McCann, and J. Marsh. 1996. *Football Violence in Europe*. Oxford: The Social Issues Research Centre.

Marx, G. T. 1970. "Issueless Riots." *Annals* 391 (September): 21–33.

McCarthy, J. D., A. Martin, and C. McPhail. 2005. "Constraints on the Freedom of Public Assembly: Police Behavior and the Demeanor of Civilians in Disorderly Campus Gatherings." Unpublished manuscript, American Sociological meetings, Philadelphia.

McPhail, C. 1971. "Civil Disorder Participation: A Critical Examination of Recent Research." *American Sociological Review* 36 (December): 1058–73.

Montreal Star. 1955. March 18, passim.

Petersilia, J., and A. Abrahamse. 1994. "A Profile of Those Arrested." In *The Los Angeles Riots: Lessons for the Urban Future*, ed. M. Baldassare, 135–47. Boulder, CO: Westview Press.

Report of the National Advisory Commission on Civil Disorders (The Kerner Report). 1968. Washington, DC: U.S. Government Printing Office.

Russell, G. W. 2004. "Sports Riots: A Social-Psychological Review." *Aggression and Violent Behavior* 9: 353–78.

Russell, G. W., and R. L. Arms. 1998. "Towards a Social Psychological Profile of Would-Be Rioters." *Aggressive Behavior* 24: 219–26.

Smelser, N. J. 1962. *Theory of Collective Behavior*. New York: The Free Press.

Sports Council/Social Science Research Council. 1978. *Public Disorder and Sporting Events*. London: Social Science Research Council.

Turner, R. 1969. "The Public Perception of Protest." *American Sociological Review* 34 (December): 815–31.

Walker, D. 1968. *Rights in Conflict*. New York: Bantam Books.

Wanderer, J. J. 1969. "An Index of Riot Severity and Some Correlates." *American Journal of Sociology* 74 (March): 500–505.

Young, K. 2002. "Standard Deviations: An Update on North American Sports Crowd Disorder." *Sociology of Sport Journal* 19:237–75.

5

Socialization of the Violent Fan: Research Questions

The previous chapter has shown that the typical individual in North America who is most accepting of fan violence and more likely to become involved in it is the young, white male. This chapter argues that sociologists and social psychologists need to think about and do research on why this is the case. The key question that must be asked is this: Are young, white males socialized into becoming violent fans? This directs us to several general issues of inquiry, including the primary and secondary socializing agents, the environments of socialization, the mechanisms of socialization, and the positive and negative outcomes of the socializing process.

To approach socialization of crowd members, it is necessary to challenge myths about crowds. This discussion of socialization assumes that crowds have a role structure and culture, and thus two prevailing myths about crowds must be challenged. The myths are (1) that crowds are "crazy" and (2) that crowds are "highly suggestible and irrational." There is no doubt that crowds commit antisocial acts. We need not look further than the Heysel Stadium soccer riot in Belgium (Lewis 1989; appendix C) to confirm this truth. But are crowds crazy? Are they out of touch with reality? Most people in crowds can recall what happened and why it happened, although they may not have liked what happened. Assuming crowds are crazy leads one to the conclusion that studying a crowd is impossible because the behavior is random and unpredictable and not amenable to scientific investigation. Collective behavior scholars reject this position. Moreover, when it is assumed that crowds have social structures with cultures, then it follows that they can be studied scientifically.

The second myth is that crowds are highly suggestible. This myth derives from the "crowds are irrational" perspective. It is a wonderful myth held by the press. Let us look at this in more detail. If crowds were as suggestible as one often sees in the newspapers, then crowd management would be very easy. All police would have to do is suggest that the crowd leave, go home, or go have a drink in the local watering hole. The police's problems would be solved for the day. However, if crowds have social structures with cultures, then one would not expect them to be highly suggestible. Any proposal likely would be dealt with by discussion with friends or peers. Any proposal or suggestion would be filtered though the person's relationships to others in the crowd. In other words, crowds should be seen as information processing entities, not emotional relay systems.

Agents of Socialization

In this section I suggest some research questions and possible lines of inquiry into the various issues of spectator socialization. It is possible to enumerate a range of agents in the socialization process for young people, including the primary agents of the family, the church, and peers. I suggest these research questions on *primary agents*:

1. How do peers participate in socializing the positive and negative aspects of fan behavior?
2. What is the place of the family in encouraging or discouraging the fan in regard to violent spectator behavior?

3. What is the place of the church in the socialization process for fan behavior?

In addition to the primary agents, there are four categories of *secondary socialization agents* that should be of interest to scholars. They are the media; popular culture; fellow spectators; and social control agents, ranging from ushers to the police, fire, and other emergency services. Questions to consider regarding these agents:

1. Is it possible to identify the point in time in a young person's life where one of the agents of socialization is more important than others?
2. How do the categories of secondary socialization agents interact?
3. Which of these categories of agents will be more effective in reducing fan violence?

I now turn to a discussion of the environments of socialization.

Environments of Socialization

The issues of the environments of socialization refer to the physical space and agents in the socialization process. Note the typology suggested in figure 5.1.

Let me discuss each cell in turn. Public space refers to locales in the Goffman (1971) sense of the term. For the study of public

	Space:		
		Public	Private
Agents:	Primary	I	II
	Secondary	III	IV

Figure 5.1.   *Socialization Agents and Public Space*

space and fan violence, the most important public places are those places where fans gather before games, the stadia where games are played, and locations where fans gather after the games are completed. To illustrate: An important before-the-game place would be bars or streets leading to the stadia, while during the games, such a gathering place might be designated locations within the stadium, such as the Dawg Pound in Cleveland or the Jungle in Cincinnati. After the game, the natural urban gathering areas would be important public spaces for fans to gather (see chapter 6).

Private space is more than a residual category for sociologists and social psychologists. It designates back regions where fans prepare for a game, watch a game on television, or gather afterward. These places might include hotel rooms, dormitory rooms, and homes.

I have already noted the distinction between primary and secondary agents of socialization. As a student of crowd behavior, I am most interested in cell III, the process of socialization by secondary agents in public space, particularly in crowds. To understand these socialization processes in sports crowd environments, it is necessary to first understand what we know theoretically and empirically about the behavior of fans. Previous chapters have addressed this issue.

Neil J. Smelser's model is presented in his book *Theory of Collective Behavior* (1962). As previously outlined, the model is divided into five determinants, each with a set of subdeterminants. The determinants are (1) structural conduciveness, (2) structural strain, (3) growth of a generalized belief, (4) mobilization for action, and (5) social control. The theory is presented in detail in chapter 2. Smelser's model suggests several questions that might be studied in terms of issues of socialization:

1. What are the structural conditions that shape agents of socialization?
2. What is the place of community problems or the culture of sport in shaping the thoughts of agents of socialization?
3. What is the place of social control agents in the socialization process?

Socialization Issues Linked to Other Theories of the Crowd

In this discussion, I treat the crowd as the independent variable socializing the fan in terms of violence. Although this book is focused primarily on North American fan violence, I will draw on work related to European soccer fan violence. To accomplish this, I will link the theoretical questions raised by the Smelser and McPhail collective behavior models to the four theoretical-empirical approaches to soccer crowds and hooliganism. These approaches are (1) the Leicester school, (2) moral panic, (3) ritualized aggression, and (4) governmental inquiries. I look at three of the Smelser determinants (structural conduciveness, strain, and social control) and the McPhail categories. I begin with the Leicester school and show its linkage to the two collective behavior models vis-à-vis the questions of fan violence socialization.

Leicester School

Over the years, the core members of the Leicester school have been very productive in writing about football. The core members are sociologists Eric Dunning and John Williams and historian Patrick Murphy. These scholars have had a number of graduate students who have extended their work. Two books—*Hooligans Abroad* (Williams, Dunning, and Murphy 1984) and *The Roots of Football Hooliganism* (Dunning, Murphy, and Williams 1988)—are exemplars of the Leicester school's scholarship. Influenced by the seminal ideas of Norbert Elias, Dunning and his colleagues argue that answers to sociological questions can only be obtained by studying long-term social processes using historical and sociological theories and data. Their claim, as related to soccer hooliganism, is germane to sports fan violence and can be summarized in four propositions:

1. Soccer hooliganism is present to a greater or lesser degree in any given time period of any professional soccer league.

2. Soccer hooliganism consists of violent acts, associated with football, of lower working-class males.
3. Soccer hooliganism is supported by a values system of aggression in lower working-class males.
4. Occupation is the best measure of social class.

For a more detailed analysis of the Leicester school see A. Bairner (2006).

With particular reference to socialization, the Leicester school directs the sociologist's attention to investigate three things in regard to structural conduciveness for crowd behavior. First, there are the historical factors that influence crowds as socializing agents. Second, there is the place of class and culture of aggression as the content of the socializing experience. Third, one must investigate occupation's influence in teaching soccer fans how to behave. In regard to structural strain, the Leicester writers tell us to look at working-class anger as reflected in the crowd. This should suggest some values that are being taught. Clearly, the Leicester school's position is arguing for an approach that emphasizes community problems in the socialization process rather than more narrow aspects of the culture of soccer. Lastly, in regard to the issue of social control (particularly formal agents), the Leicester school provides little direction.

Turning to the McPhail categories, there are no suggestions on what students of crowds should pay attention to in terms of appropriate and inappropriate. What is the appropriate and inappropriate behavior that is socialized in the crowd context? The Leicester position argues that it has a working-class content. Thus, we can ask if there are McPhail categories, such as vocalization and grasping, lifting, waving, that have uniquely working-class origins.

Moral Panic

Stanley Cohen (1972), an English sociologist who studies deviance, developed the idea of moral panic in his research on English youth gangs. He describes a moral panic as a situation where societies define a "condition, episode, person or group, as a threat to societal values and interests" (Cohen 1972, 1). He gives particular power to the media's role in spreading the moral panic through a process that he calls deviance amplification. The media set the agenda for discourse by identifying who the "folk devils" are in any particular time or place in society and what is morally wrong about their behavior.

Moral panic and Smelser's structural conduciveness point to the media as a primary socializing agent. One theoretical problem is how to link the media with the training of behavior in the context of the crowd. One possible way is to see if the media provide any specific instructions for the supporters at a particular event. For example, in the Cleveland beer riot, the media encouraged fans to come down to the stadium and attack the Texas Rangers baseball team.

It is possible that some actions described by the McPhail categories are more likely to be interpreted as moral panic than others. For example, certain collective vocalizations might generate more criticisms, and hence, moral panic, than would actions described as grasping, lifting, and waving. Perhaps sociologists need to specifically define distribution of behaviors that are generally defined by the various agencies as morally repugnant.

Ritualized Aggression

The ritual violence and aggression position has been articulated in the work of Peter Marsh (1982) and was very influential in the 1970s and early 1980s but seems no longer to be an important force in the efforts to understand soccer hooliganism. The theory of ritualized aggression argues that soccer hooliganism is governed by a set of rules, and that most of it is designed not to harm but to humiliate the opponent. It is further argued that this violence is simply an expression of ritual aggression that can be observed in a variety of nonhuman species. The data of the ritual approach are obtained from field work at soccer stadia and from interviews with hooligans about the interpretive rule of the aggression.

Ritualized aggression would take the position under Smelser's structural conduciveness that the conditions for crowd violence will be the same across any given population. Given the size of the United States and its diverse populations, the ritualized aggression position would say that fan behavior that is violent would be shaped only by the culture of the sport and no other conditions such as community problems. Further, strain would be linked to the culture of the sport, particularly winning and losing, and not to broader social conditions. Social control is particularly important as the crowd socializes in the ritualized aggression position since the police and other agents create the area for the aggression to occur. The ritualized aggression is clearly linked to the McPhail analysis because it argues that there are scripts which all the actors know and agree to. Thus, the sociologist, using the McPhail categories, needs to determine which actions described by the McPhail categories are acceptable and which are not. For example, when or where does the script call for vocalization, such as chanting "Bullshit, bullshit"?

Government Inquires

Since the mid-1960s, British soccer has had a number of tragedies associated with it. Venues such as Bradford, Birmingham, Hillsborough, Heysel, and Ibrox have become symbols for soccer horrors. Some of these tragedies were directly related to soccer hooliganism (Heysel; see appendix C), while others were indirectly related (Bradford and Hillsborough). The causes of, as well as the solutions to, soccer hooliganism have been widely debated (Taylor 1990). Whatever the cause or solution, hooliganism has had a profound effect on English soccer, ranging from major changes in architecture of stadia to the selling of programs. At least nine reports have been published in the last thirty years. These reports have described the official view of the causes of the disaster and have offered many recommendations for the improvement of safety and better crowd-control strategies in English football stadia. Let's take a look at the typical elements of one of these official reports.

After each football tragedy, an inquiry chairperson was appointed and instructed to immediately investigate the causes of the disaster and make recommendations as to the future of sports. These inquiries typically issue reports which have wide-ranging impacts on policy making, as well as guiding research. It is usual to find a wide-ranging policy mandate in these reports. For example, Lord Taylor was instructed to conduct an inquiry into the Hillsborough tragedy and "make recommendations about the needs of crowd control and safety at sports events" (Taylor 1990, 1). The content presented in the official reports is more legal than behavioral (Lewis and Scarisbrick-Hauser 1994). For example, the McPhail categories rarely appear in any form in these reports. The Hillsborough final report presented by Lord Taylor devotes only ten pages to the events of the Hillsborough disaster, although the interim report has more detailed coverage of the disaster. The remainder of the report is concerned with future crowd-control strategies and crowd safety at sports events. The major weakness of government inquires is that they are void of any sociological theory. For some, that is a strength in that it leads to objectivity. Government inquiries direct the analyst to look at the demographics of hooliganism, particularly such factors as race, genders, and religion and can be linked to both structural conduciveness and strain. These government reports also provide good information on the activities of the police and other social control agents

A Theory of Sports Fan Socialization

It is now possible to propose a theory of sports fan crowd socialization based on the material in the previous sections of this chapter. This theory is expressed in the following propositions:

1. Violent fans are more likely to be socialized in public space than private space.
2. Violent fans are more likely to be socialized by secondary socializing agents than primary agents.
3. The greater the number of males in a crowd, the more likely the acceptance of crowd violence.
4. As a sports crowd becomes more diverse on the basis of gender, the less likely will be the occurence of violence.

5. There is a direct correlation between the importance of the competition and the socialization processes of the crowd.
6. Beliefs governing the acceptance of crowd violence are more prevalent in lower- and working-class cultures.
7. There is an inverse relationship between crowd violence perceived as ritualistic and social class.
8. Sports crowds will differentiate into social roles when socializing violent behavior.
9. Sports crowd behaviors are ranked from acceptable to unacceptable by differing agencies on basis of a crowd cultures—the greater the level of acceptance, the greater the level of perceived ritualized aggression.
10. The greater the number of social control agents, the more likely crowd violence will be perceived as ritualistic.

Socialization and Triangulation

In this section I propose a research strategy related to fan violence. It is an extension of material on triangulation presented in chapter 3. To briefly review: Triangulation is defined as the use of multiple research methods, in coordination, to answer sociological questions. The strategy proposed here is based on my experiences studying American sports crowds and English soccer crowds (Lewis 1982). There are two types of triangulation. The first uses primary data, in which the researcher records observations and carries out personal interviews. The other uses secondary data which the researcher obtains by collecting information from sources such as newspapers, magazine articles, films, and police documents.

Using the hypothetical case vignette for football developed for the experiment in chapter 4, it is possible to generate triangulation questions. Here is the hypothetical vignette:

City and state police and the National Guard were mobilized last night as football fans became destructive. Looting, fire, and vandalism went unchecked for hours as the authorities battled the crowd in an attempt to eliminate gunfire and restore order.

Damage was estimated in the hundreds of thousands of dollars. Two people were killed (a fan and a police officer). Numerous injuries were also reported.

In regard to *interviews*, the researcher might ask such questions as, Where did you talk about celebrating the victory—in a bar, at the game, or at a party in residence or dorm room? With whom did you talk? Did anyone encourage or discourage you from going somewhere to celebrate a victory? Did you go to the crowd celebration with anyone else? Using *site visits*, the scholar would see if the physical space where the crowd gathered would be likely to facilitate conversation and, hence, socialization. In regard to *newspaper and magazine* articles, the sociologist would use questions to determine if people assembled for crowd actions by themselves or with others. Sociologists would look at *photographs and films* to find clusters of people, assuming that the clusters of people in the crowd would likely know each other and thus socialization would be facilitated. Lastly, *police documents* could be used to get at the demographics of the crowd, suggesting that if the crowd had similar demographics this would facilitate socialization.

In the next chapter, using the intensive case history method, the analysis looks at two celebrating riots involving young people, and primarily young, white males: the 2002 Ohio State football riot and the 2004 Red Sox baseball riot.

References

Cohen, S. 1972. *Folk, Devils, and Moral Panics*. London: MacGibbon and Kee.

Dunning, E., P. Murphy, and J. Williams. 1988. *The Roots of Football Hooliganism: An Historical and Sociological Study*. London: Routledge & Kegan Paul.

Goffman, E. 1971. *Relations in Public*. New York: Basic Books.

Lewis, J. M. 1982. "Crowd Control at English Soccer Matches." *Sociological Focus* 15: 417–23.

———. 1989. "A Value-Added Analysis of the Heysel Riot." *Current Psychology* 8 (1): 15–29.

Lewis, J. M., and A. Scarisbrick-Hauser. 1994. "An Analysis of Football Crowd Safety Reports Using the McPhail Categories." In *Football, Violence, and Social Identity*, ed. R. Giulianotti, N. Bonney, and M. Hepworth, chap. 7 (pp. 158–73). London: Routledge.

Marsh, P. 1982. *Aggro: The Illusion of Violence*. Oxford: Basil Blackwell.

McPhail, C. 1991. *The Myth of the Madding Crowd*. New York: Aldine De Gruyter.

Smelser, N. J. 1962. *Theory of Collective Behavior*. New York: The Free Press.

Taylor, P. (Lord Justice). 1990. *Inquiry into the Hillsborough Stadium Disaster*. Final report. London: Her Majesty's Stationery Office.

Williams, J., E. Dunning, and P. Murphy. 1984. *Hooligans Abroad: The Behaviour and Control of English Football Fans in Continental Europe*. London: Routledge & Kegan Paul.

6

The Ohio State and Red Sox Celebrating Riots[1]

This chapter, in contrast to chapter 4, takes a micro approach to the problem of sports fan violence by studying two celebrating riots. It uses the intensive case history method (see chapter 3) to examine the celebrating riots associated with the Ohio State football victory over Michigan in 2002 and the Boston Red Sox victory over the New York Yankees in 2004. This chapter is divided into five sections. The first section poses a theoretical model for looking at celebrating riots. This is followed, in turn, by a narrative of the riots, a discussion of the research methodology, an analysis of the riots, and conclusions. To review, a celebrating sports riot is defined as five or more individuals, at a sporting event attended by at least one hundred fans, using any or all of the following types of violence to celebrate a sports victory: vandalism, throwing missiles, rushing playing fields or courts, arson, and fighting with other fans or social control forces. I suggest you consult Kevin Young (2002) for an excellent review of the literature on the actual behavior of violent fans.

Many of the individulas who carry out celebrating riots are college and university students. Cynthia Buettner (2004, 139–40), in a survey of thirty-one major universities, found that twenty-one universities (68 percent) reported that they had celebrating riots within the last ten years. The riot populations were large, having a mean of 3,104 people and a range of 300 to 10,000 people, and surveys showed March and November as having the most frequent riots reported (Buettner 2004, 142). No demographic data were reported from the surveys, except for student status.

In the fall of 2002, several celebrating riots happened during and after the Ohio State–Michigan football game, which Ohio State University (OSU) won. The OSU events were some of the most serious riots ever to occur after a college football game and certainly the most serious in the long history of the Ohio State–Michigan rivalry.

A Theory of Celebrating Riots

Celebrating violence after major sporting events is likely to occur when certain conditions are present. My research (Lewis 1982, 1989, 2002), as well as my students' research (Dugan 1988; Ward 2002; Ward, Lewis, and Benson 2002), has shown that celebrating sports riots are becoming a part of the North American sports scene at both the collegiate and professional levels of competition (see chapter 4).

In December 2002, I proposed the initial version of a theory of celebrating riots to the *New York Times* (Gettleman 2002). It is an extension of both the Smelser (1962) and McPhail (1991) approaches to fan violence. What follows is a more developed version of the celebrating riots theory. This theory is empirically derived and is less macro than Smelser's theory but more macro that McPhail's ideas approach to crowd behavior. I argue that the major type of sports fan violence in the United States is the celebrating riot. It should be noted that Young (2002, 274) prefers the term *post-event riot* to celebrating riot. While it is true that some post-event riots are carried out by the fans of the losing team after championship play, I still prefer the concept of "celebrating riot."

Celebrating violence after major sporting events is likely to occur when certain conditions are present. These conditions can be expressed in terms of the following hypotheses.

1. *A celebrating sports riot by fans of the winning team is more likely than a punishing riot by fans of the losing team.* The rioting is done in celebration of a victory by the fans of the winning team. Here we have sharp contrast with soccer hooliganism in Britain. Soccer hooliganism in Britain, particularly England, tends to be initiated by the fans of the losing team against the supporters of the winning team. What often happens is that some fans of the losing team try to catch fans of the winning who are heading for buses or trains and give them a "punch up." It should be noted that there have been a few exceptions in the United States, most notably at Michigan State in March 1999 (Kaplowitz and Campo 2004), when the violence was carried out by the fans of the losing team.

2. *A celebrating sports riot is more likely to occur after championship games.* Championship play is important because of the stress we put on winning in American society, particularly on high-level competition, which the Bowl Championship Series (BCS) certainly represents.

3. *A celebrating sports riot is more likely to occur if the winning team has not won a championship within five years.* This factor also links to the importance of winning in major sports championships in American society. For any Division I football team, there are two important championships: the conference championship and a bowl victory. Further, in recent years, college football has developed the BCS to pick a Division I collegiate football champion. The BCS champion is based on complicated computer rankings as well as a formal competition with the top two teams playing a bowl game at the beginning of the new year. The longer a team has gone without winning a championship, the more important the winning becomes and the more likely that there will be fan violence when the team does win an important victory.

A championship within the last five years seems to have a calming effect on the fans of the winning team. This five-year factor seems to be true for all sports. Thus, if teams have had a championship within recent times, fans are less likely to riot in celebration of the current victory.

Traditional rivalries are games between opponents that have a history of competition that is deemed by fans and the media as being championship-like, games that are very important to win, or to not lose. For example, in collegiate football, the annual Ohio State–Michigan game is seen by some as the most important traditional rivalry. Others would note the Army-Navy game. In professional baseball an important rivalry is the New York Yankees–Boston Red Sox competition.

4. *A celebrating sports riot is more likely the deeper into the championship series play continues.* This hypothesis does not apply to football since competition is not organized around a multigame series in the same way as the baseball, basketball, and hockey championships. The reason that celebrating riots are more likely to occur deeper in a series is that the culture of winning has been developing over the days or weeks of the competition. Fans have been talking about the events of the competition, thus increasing the importance of the events.

The closer a series goes toward the last game of the series, the more likely there is to be sports fan violence by the fans of the winning team. For example, in baseball, basketball, and hockey series, which are scheduled for seven games, the likelihood of fan violence increases if the series goes to the sixth or seventh game.

5. *A celebrating sports riot is more likely to occur if the concluding game is a close, exciting event.* That is, for instance, a game in which one score would determine the winner. For football, the score might be an extra point, a safety, a field goal, or a touchdown. These factors—a close score and lots of excitement— prepare the way for celebrating fan violence. A close, exciting victory is more likely to encourage a celebrating riot than a victory that is not close and exciting. Not all sports victories that are close are also exciting, but when competition creates a situation of suspense as to the final outcome then there is the potential for fan violence.

6. *A celebrating sports riot is facilitated by sports fans' access to a natural urban gathering area.* Beginning with the Chicago School

of Sociology, "place" has been an important aspect of urban sociology. Anthony Orum (1998) argues that urban sociologists have looked at physical space or place in three ways. The first way space is looked at is as a location of hope and aspiration. It is the venue where people hope to create a new life. The second way space is used is as a community. Large cities have urban spaces where people can live out much of their work, education, and recreation lives. Lastly, says Orum, there are areas which are specific, concrete expressions of community space. These are places one can return to as the old "neighborhood." Natural urban gathering places in most big cities have all three types of spaces. They are areas where people want to be seen and to see others on the street. By *natural* I mean that in the organization of the city, these areas are seen as gathering places (McPhail 1991) where crowds assemble for a number of reasons, quite independent of fan violence, including festivals, shopping, and parades. It is easy to access these places because they are typically in reach of major sports venues via walking and/or public transportation. For example, in Chicago many areas of Michigan Avenue would qualify as natural urban gathering areas. In Cleveland the Flats would meet the standard of place. Other examples include Boston's Kenmore Square, Columbus, Ohio's High Street, Pittsburgh's Triangle area, and New York's Central Park.

Some questions are suggested: Why do natural urban gathering places facilitate fan violence? Could the urban gathering place be seen as a field of play, thus furthering the identification of the rioter with the athlete? Should police and other social control forces take an aggressive stand and put their personnel in these natural urban gathering places? How does attacking the goalposts in a football game or rushing the court in a basketball game relate to the space of the natural urban gathering place? Some of these questions are dealt with in the next chapter.

7. *If a celebrating riot occurs, the typical rioter will likely be a young, white male.* As I noted in chapter 4, age and gender are the two basic predictors of who is likely to participate in a riot. This holds true for celebrating fan violence. Both British and American researchers have written that the typical sports rioter is a young, white male. Why young, white males rather than other

demographic social roles? We can answer this question by elimination. Older people simply do not riot in almost any circum-
stance. It is not part of the social role of women to get involved
in sports riots. Indeed, they would likely be highly discouraged
by parents and significant others from doing so. Both male and
female Blacks say it is not worth the risk for black males to get
involved in a sports riot because of the higher probability they
will be picked up and arrested by police for reasons of visibility
and cultural history.

I have eliminated other demographic categories as violent
fans, yet the young, white male remains. Why? The reason lies in
the strong identification with the victory experience. The violent
fan wants to be part of the victory, yet he cannot throw a football
fifty yards or dunk a basketball. But he can be violent. It is possible that the young, white male commits fan violence (vandalism, throwing missiles, fighting, etc.) as an imagined feat of skill
to identify with the collegiate or professional athletes who have
exhibited their skill at a football, basketball, baseball, or hockey
game.

I now turn to an examination of two celebrating sports riots
that involved young, white males, many of whom were college
and university students.

Data Sources

For writing convenience I refer to the two riots as the Ohio
State riot and the Red Sox riot. However, it should be noted
that each riot involved another team—Michigan for football
and the Yankees for baseball.

Researchers have various ways for collecting data for the
studies they conduct. I studied the Ohio State and Red Sox celebrating riots using the triangulation for collecting data. In chapter 3, I suggested that triangulation was based on five sources
(methods) of data collection that can be used to investigate
sports riots: site visits, personal interviews, newspaper accounts,
photographs and films, and police documents.

Site Visits

A researcher is rarely present at the scene of a sports riot; hence, he or she must reconstruct the riot behavior. In this particular research, while I was not at the actual riot, I am familiar with Ohio Stadium and the surrounding area, having been on the Ohio State campus on many occasions. I revisited the site in the spring of 2004. In regard to Boston, I lived, as a graduate student, near the site of the celebrating riot and revisited it in the spring of 2005.

Personal Interviews

There are two types of interviews: one that the scholar completes personally, and one that he or she obtains from secondary sources, particularly newspapers. I interviewed two eyewitness to the Ohio State riot.[2] Lastly, it should noted that I was an "eyewitnesses" to this riot as I was watching the broadcast of the game on television. I did not do personal interviews for the Red Sox riot.

Newspaper Accounts

For the Ohio State research, I used accounts from four Ohio newspapers—the *Akron Beacon Journal* (Akron area), the *Columbus Dispatch* (Columbus area), the *Lantern* (the OSU newspaper, Columbus), and the *Record Courier* (Kent area). These papers provided material from reporters and photographers at the game. For the Red Sox riot, I drew on the following papers: the *Boston Herald*, the *Boston Globe*, the *Chicago Sun-Times*, and *USA Today*.

Photographs and Films

To facilitate this research I used photographs from newspapers and watched film versions from local and national television reports of both riots, including *CBS News* and ESPN's *Sports Center*.

Police Documents

Police documents are helpful in informing a researcher about the amount and location of officers, how many arrests were made, and the types of violence that occurred. I was able to obtain information from the Public Information Office of the Columbus Division of Police on those who were arrested during the Ohio State riot segments. There were no police documents available to me for the Red Sox riot.

Riot Narratives

Ohio State

In the fall of 2002 a set of celebrating riots took place after the Ohio State–Michigan football game that OSU won. The riots were the most serious in the long history of what has been described by ESPN as college football's greatest rivalry (Phillips 2002). The riots began in the afternoon of November 23 and ended in the early hours of November 24. By many measures that was one of the most serious riots ever to occur after a college football game.

There were three different crowd actions in three different venues that make up this event that falls under the rubric of the "Ohio State celebrating riots." The riots ended what was known on the Ohio State campus as "Beat Michigan week" (Buettner 2004, 114). The first event occurred after Ohio State won the game in the last play. Fans rushed the field attacking the south goalpost. Police responded by spraying pepper gas on the attackers who were primarily young, white males.

One eyewitness told me that at first the police were trying to keep the fans off the field, but changed the strategy, "calling an audible," in the words of the eyewitness, and letting the fans go on the field (D. Lewis, interview). Fans headed for the south post and attempted to tear it down. Police fought off the fans around the goalposts with pepper spray, and fans threw clods of dirt at the police. Eventually, police gave up trying to stop the fans. The goalposts, however, did not come down because of the posts' stability and the aggressive actions of the police.

The second and third phases of the crowd actions took place in the University District. The second phase was located primarily on High Street approximately a mile from Ohio Stadium where the game had been played. Most of the activity here was boisterous yelling and chanting. There was very little violence in this phase of the crowd actions.

The third phase began around midnight in the area of 13th Avenue about three blocks southeast from the edge of the Ohio State campus. There were eight "hot spots" which the *Columbus Dispatch* identified as riot locations (Dutton 2002). The activity in this crowd action involved violence, including throwing missiles at police, setting cars on fire (estimates range from ten to twenty cars set on fire), window breakage, streetlights torn down, and vandalism. The crowd action began about midnight and came to a resolution about 4 a.m. on November 24, 2002 (Buettner 2004, 106). To control this crowd action, police used tear gas and wooden pellets known as "knee-knockers" to control and disperse the crowd. Heat from the car fires was so intense that 13th Avenue had to be closed (McCarthy 2002).

As true of most riots, there were several reports of citations and arrests. Initially, there were at least three figures on arrests. The Columbus police department uses the figure of 49; the *Columbus Dispatch*, 58; and OSU, 67. On December 6, 2002, the OSU administration listed a final figure for people cited or arrested in connection with the celebration disturbances as 70, with 17 OSU students (23 percent) being among those charged (Task Force 2003, 25). The estimated damage has never been reported although several reports indicated that at least twenty cars were damaged or destroyed.

The Red Sox[3]

Since 1918, the Boston Red Sox have appeared in five World Series and have lost all of them, until now. In 1919 the Boston Red Sox sold Babe Ruth to the Yankees and after that, some people credited their continuous bad luck to "the curse of the Bambino."

The playoffs were very intense, with Boston losing three in a row to the Yankees before coming back for an unbelievable victory in the last four games. This was the first time in history that a team had won four in a row to win the championship. The energy that the Boston players had was almost as though it came straight out of a Hollywood baseball movie. Some players went on the field with injuries, but they just had to finish the game. That last game of the series on October 20, 2004, however, was very exciting for the fans as well as the players. Once that last out was called, Boston fans all over started to celebrate. However, for some, the celebration turned into violence.

Crowds began to gather after the victory. In Boston it was estimated that, at its height, the crowd reached eighty thousand. Some of the celebrators were college students. The Red Sox's Fenway Park is surrounded by student housing, primarily for Boston University and Emerson College, but also for students from nearby schools such as MIT (Massachusetts Institute of Technology) and Northeastern. Around Fenway Park the streets are lined with nightclubs and bars so the celebrating becomes a little easier for some people in the area, especially students. The celebration turned into vandalism and a primarily young rowdy crowd starting to become deviant. The police started to clear out Kenmore Square and Lansdowne Street at about 1:00 a.m. Kenmore Square was clearing out, but trouble really began to arise at Lansdowne Street and Brookline Avenue in front of Fenway Park.

On Lansdowne Street people were trying to climb the steel structures behind the Green Monster of Fenway. This led to the police officers shooting FN303 pepper ball guns into the crowd. Once the officers started to shoot, people started to throw bottles at the officers, making the situation even more dangerous. During this exchange, nearby streets started to flood with people celebrating by throwing toilet paper into the streets and jumping on top of cars. Many people described the scene as wild and chaotic.

The police made efforts to get the crowd away, and then there was a scream. Victoria Snelgrove, standing near the Green Monster wall of Fenway Park, was hit in the eye with a pepper gun ball and was rushed to the hospital, but died Thursday morning. She was a 21–year-old Emerson College journalism major, whose birthday was the following Friday. For some, the curse of the Bambino was never really broken.

Analysis

I now turn to an analysis using the seven hypotheses proposed earlier in the chapter and I will apply them to the Ohio State and Red Sox celebrating riots.

1. *A celebrating sports riot is more likely by fans of the winning team than punishing riots by fans of the losing team.* Both riots were carried out by fans of the winning team. There is no evidence that either Michigan (Ohio State) or Yankee (Red Sox) fans were involved in the celebrating riots.[4] For the Ohio State riot I examined photographs, arrest statistics, and personal accounts, and nowhere is there any evidence that Michigan fans participated in the riots. Some Michigan fans were subjected to insults during the game, but this would not be considered celebrating fan violence.

For the Red Sox riot there is, again, no evidence that fans from the opposing team participated in the riot. This conclusion is supported by an examination of published photographs and newspaper accounts of the riot.

Indeed, in both celebrating riots there were no reports of any attacks on Michigan or Yankee fans. In both cases the "opponents" for the fans were the police and other emergency services.

2. *A celebrating sports riot is more likely to occur after championship games.* Championship play is important because of the stress American society and particularly sports fans put on winning. Consider the Green Bay Packers' coach Vince Lombardi's famous aphorism, "Winning isn't everything; it's the only thing." College football fans have embraced the importance of

the BCS as representing the road to the national championship in Division I collegiate football.

The Ohio State–Michigan game was a championship game in two ways. A win over Michigan guaranteed two things. First, and mostly importantly, it would put Ohio State in the championship game of the BCS, which would allow them to compete for the national title. The opponent in that game, to be held in the Fiesta Bowl, would most likely be Miami, who had been at the top of the BCS rankings for most of the collegiate football season. (As it turned out, the win did put OSU into the BCS championship with Miami.)

The second aspect of the championship play involved the Big Ten football title. An Ohio State win would put them into a tie with the University of Iowa for the Big Ten title. This is a very prestigious title in the culture of Division I football.

Lastly, while not championship play per se, a victory over Michigan in a very traditional rival would make the season for Ohio State. ESPN has described this game as college football's best rivalry, noting that the teams have met continuously since 1918. Further, since 1935, the game has been the last game for each team in the conference season. Indeed, some in the football culture have referred to the Big Ten as really the "Big Two" and the "Little Eight (Nine)."

In regard to the Boston Red Sox riot, the World Series is the most important event in professional baseball. To get to the World Series, the playoffs are crucial. The Boston Red Sox were playing the last playoff game on October 20, 2004, against the New York Yankees. If Boston won this game, not only would they be able to go to the World Series, but they would be the 2004 American League champions. The pressure to succeed was immense, not only for the players, but for the fans.

Much of this pressure could be linked to the "curse of the Bambino" and the need for the Boston fans to prove that this curse was over. The curse came about because Babe Ruth was traded by the Red Sox to the Yankees. People believed it was because of that terrible trade that Boston had lost so many games for so long. Since 1919 this curse has caused every Boston team to lose, and lose by making simple mistakes. They would miss an easy play, like a grounder in between the legs, or give up hits. These 2004 fans were deeply concerned with the thought of another hard loss. Most fans really want their team to win, and they often feel stress for their team to win; however, your average fan does not feel the pressure of "the curse." People all over the country watched this playoff game on television and felt the pressure of the curse. Everyone watched, waiting for something bad to happen to the Red Sox, fearing that after all these years, maybe the curse really is real.

In addition to the curse, there are some real hard facts that caused Boston fans to be concerned about the American League Championship games. First, Boston was down 0–3 in the series, which meant that a Yankee victory in the next game would clinch the series and advance them to the World Series. Boston faced impossible odds. Never in the history of the game has a team come back from being down 0–3 in a series to win. However, this happened, and the Red Sox earned a seventh and deciding playoff game with the Yankees.

Some had suggested that because of the team's history of losing and the curse of the Bambino, Boston fans were not typical fans. They wanted the victory more than followers of other sports teams. Thus, this was not an average championships; it was far more serious. The Boston Red Sox fans were ready to win, to celebrate and celebrate big.

3. *A celebrating sports riot is more likely to occur if the winning team has not won a championship within five years.* This factor also links to the importance of winning in major sports championships in American society. For any major collegiate football team, there are two important championships—the bowl championship, which is based on complicated computer rankings as well as a formal competition with the top two teams playing a bowl game at the beginning of the new year. Also, there is the league championship. The longer a team has gone without winning a championship the more important the winning becomes. Ohio State had not won a national championship since 1968 and a Big Ten championship outright since 1984, although it had shared the title with Michigan in 1986, Wisconsin in 1993, and Northwestern in 1996. So the drought of championships was

thirty-four years for a national championship and eighteen years for an outright Big Ten championship.

Turning to the Red Sox, since 1918 the Boston Red Sox had appeared in five World Series and lost all of them. The 2004 victory would be the first Boston win since the curse of the Bambino began. Since Boston had lost for so long, the self-worth of the Boston ball club was continually lowered. After so many crucial losses, it is hard for a team to believe that they are going to win this time around. The fans began to have the same emotional feelings for their team. When Boston won, the fans reacted not only because they won after so many long years, but because it proved that the curse was over. If the curse was over, then Boston could continue to win championships.

The reality is that the World Series is the most important event in baseball, and to win this was exciting not only for the teams playing and their fans, but for all Americans. When Boston fans won, they "proved" to America how great the Sox really were as a team. Because it took so long for the Red Sox to win the championship, it was extremely important to the Boston fans once their team did win.

4. *A celebrating sports riot is more likely the deeper the series goes into the championship.* Since this hypothesis does not apply to football, as competition is not organized around multigame series, we will not discuss the Ohio State riot here.

Turning to the Red Sox, if the Sox beat the Yankees and later won the World Series, there could be no better sense of closure. It is because of the Yankees that "the curse" even existed. People recognized the Yankees for being an unbeatable team because they have won so many championships. When watching this last playoff game for the American League Championship it was as though it was a movie. The underdog was finally going to win. Even if you did not like Boston there was a good chance that you wanted them to win just so you could see the Yankees lose.

The Yankees won the first three games of the series making it look like the team was a lock to win the American League and a place in the World Series. However, Boston won the next four games and made it into the World Series, and the celebrating began.

5. *A celebrating sports riot is more likely to occur if the concluding game is a close, exciting event.* A celebrating sports riot is more likely to occur if the game is close—that is, where one score would determine the winner—than in a game that is one-sided, or where the action is uneventful.

The Ohio State–Michigan game was a prototypical example of a close, exciting game. With fifty-eight seconds remaining and Ohio State winning 14–9, Michigan got the ball on its own twenty yard line. It began a drive and reached the Ohio State twenty-four yard line, when the Michigan quarterback was intercepted on a third-and-ten play with one second remaining. The game could not have been more exciting for both sets of football fans. Almost immediately after the interception, Ohio State fans begin to rush the field.

In contrast, the Red Sox easily won the seventh (final) game of the American League Championship Series (ALCS). Indeed, it approached a blow out, with the Red Sox leading by a score of 8–3 going into the eighth inning. The Sox then scored a run in the eighth and another in the ninth, winning the final game of the ALCS by a score of 10–3. Thus, "closeness" was not a factor in the riot.

6. *A celebrating sports riot is facilitated by sports fans' access to a natural urban gathering area.* The Ohio State riots took place within easy walking distance of the Ohio Stadium (Buettner 2004, 104). The first, of course, took place in the stadium. The second took place primarily on High Street in an area across from the Ohio State University main campus. I walked the distance from the stadium to this area in about twelve minutes. The third crowd action took place primarily on 13th Avenue, which is three blocks southeast of the stadium.

As noted earlier, the Boston fans had easy access to bars in the area near Kenmore Square. This is a quick walk from many college campuses.

7. *If a celebrating riot occurs, the typical rioter will likely be a young, white male.* Both British and American researchers have

written that the typical sports rioter is a young, white male. These patterns were reviewed in chapter 4.

In regard to the Ohio State riot, I was able to develop two sets of evidence that suggest that the Ohio State rioters were primarily young, white males. (See chapter 4.) First, using the *Columbus Dispatch* arrest data (N = 57) forty-eight of those arrested had male names, seven had female names, and two had names that could have been male or female (*Columbus Dispatch* 2002). Of the forty-eight males, the mean age was 22.6 years, with the range of 17–40. Thus, it can be concluded that of those arrested, the typical rioter was a young, white male. (While race is difficult to determine from names by inspection, it can be tentatively concluded that those arrested were not African American or Asian.) The Ohio State University *Final Report* (Task Force 2003, 28) indicated that all of the Ohio State students arrested in postgame disturbances were male. Further, the report stated that "by self-report and by police report [none] were intoxicated." While there are few exceptions in the United States, notably Michigan State after losing basketball games in 1999 and 2002, most violence at both the collegiate and professional levels of sport competition is carried out by the fans of the winning team.

My research assistant and I looked at photographs of the rioters at both the attack on the goalposts and the burning of cars on 13th Avenue. We examined the photographs independently and concluded that most of the individuals in the photographs were young, white males carrying out the action of the riot, that is, attacking the goalposts, setting couches on fire, or burning cars.

In regard to the Red Sox riot, photographic evidence shows that most of those involved were young, white males. Based on initial reports, those arrested in the Kenmore Square–Fenway Park area were all males ranging from age nineteen to thirty-eight. There were a good number of women in the crowd, but most were spectators like Victoria Snelgrove, who tragically was killed.

Summary and Conclusions

In summary, these two intensive case histories provide some support for the proposed theory of celebrating riots. Indeed, the only factor missing was the fact that Boston won the last game of the ALCS over the Yankees by a lopsided score; the game was not a close, exciting event. All the other variables suggested by the theory were supported.

It becomes necessary to move beyond case histories to determine the extent that this theory holds true. Further, some of the variables need further study, most notably the selective participation of young, white males in the rioting process. The most pressing research question is, Why is this category of individuals more likely to celebrate a victory by rioting in a crowd than other categories of sports fans? More about research on sports fan violence will be discussed in chapter 8.

In the next chapter I analyze how societies, or at least significant segments of society, deal with serious fan violence that becomes polluting to society itself.

Notes

1. I wish to thank Sarah Harkness, my research assistant, for her work on the Ohio State riot aspects of this chapter.

2. One interview, on November 25, 2002, was with Damon Lewis, my son, who was at the game in Columbus. The other interview was with an Ohio State student who was a friend of one of my Kent State students and who wished not to be identified by name.

3. The initial draft of this narrative was written by one of my students, Desiree Rodriguez. Miss Rodriguez wrote the draft, for academic credit, when she was one of my collective behavior students at Hiram College.

4. There is one mention that an Ohio State graduate who taught at Michigan saw four Michigan students overturning a car, but this report was never mentioned again after the initial story.

References

Bairner, A. 2006. "The Leicester School and the Study of Football Hooliganism." *Sport in Society* 9 (October) no. 4, 583–98.

Buettner, C. K. 2004. "Parties, Police, and Pandemonium: An Exploratory Study of Mixed Issue Campus Disturbances." PhD dissertation, The Ohio State University.

Columbus Dispatch. 2002. "Riot Charges." November 26, 4A. www.dispatch.com.

Dugan, K. 1988. "An Analysis of the World Series Celebrating Riots Using Smelser's Structural Conduciveness." MA thesis, Kent State University, Kent, OH.

Dutton, G. 2002. "City, OSU Vow to Punish All Who Broke the Law; of 48 Cited, Only 7 Were Students." *Columbus Dispatch*, November 25. www.dispatch.com.

Gettleman, J. 2002. "A Fall Tradition: Rooting and Rioting for the Home Team." *New York Times*, December 1, 4-2.

Kaplowitz, S., and S. Campo. 2004. "Drinking Alcohol Policy, and Attitudes toward a Campus Riot." *Journal of College Student Development* 45, no. 5 (September/October): 1–10.

Lewis, J. M. 1982. "Fan Violence: An American Social Problem." In *Research in Social Problems and Public Policy*, ed. M. Lewis, vol. 2, 175–206. Greenwich, CT: JAI Press.

———. 1989. "A Value-Added Analysis of the Heysel Stadium Soccer Riot." *Current Psychology* 8 (1): 15–29.

———. 2002. "The Cleveland Beer Bottle Riot." American Sociological Association meetings.

McCarthy, J. 2002. "Rowdy Fans Tarnish Bucks Win." *Dayton Daily News*, November 25, A1, A8.

McPhail, C. 1991. *The Myth of the Madding Crowd.* New York: Aldine de Gruyter.

Orum, A. M. 1998. "The Urban Imagination of Sociologists: The Centrality of Place." *Sociological Quarterly* 39 (1): 1–10.

Phillips, L. 2002 "Ohio State vs. Michigan: College Football's Best Rivalry." Gannett News Service. www.centralohio.com/ohiostate/football/legacy/Michigan/part1.html.

Smelser, N. J. 1962. *Theory of Collective Behavior.* New York: The Free Press.

Task Force on Preventing Celebratory Riots (Task Force). 2003. *Final Report.* Columbus: The Ohio State University.

Ward, R. E. 2002. "Fan Violence Social Problem or Moral Panic?" *Aggression and Violent Behavior* 2: 453–75.

Ward, R. E., J. M. Lewis, and D. E. Benson. 2002. "Sports Officials' Judgements of Spectator Behavior: A Factorial Survey." *Michigan Sociological Review* 16 (Fall): 147–70.

Young, K. 2002. "Standard Deviations: An Update on North American Sports Crowd Disorder." *Sociology of Sport Journal* 19: 237–75.

7

Serious Fan Violence and the Importance of Sport

In chapter 7 I build on the analysis of the Ohio State and Red Sox riots in the previous chapter to show how serious fan violence harms society and sport. Further, I discuss the ritual responses to serious fan violence as elements in society respond to this violence.

Serious Fan Violence and the Functions of Sport

It has been argued by sport sociologists (Coakley and Dunning 2000, part 1), generally writing from a structural functional position, that sport, particularly organized sport, has a range of functions for society. Loy and Booth (2000, 12–16) summarize the work of many structural-functionalists. A useful functional analysis is one proposed by Stevenson and Nixon (as cited in Loy and Booth 2000, 15) suggesting that sport has five functions for society:

1. Socio-emotional
2. Socialization
3. Integrative
4. Political
5. Social mobility

The *socio-emotional* function of sport contributes to the psychological health of society. It has been argued that sport serves to reduce aggression by allowing people to act out their aggressive feelings through the playing or watching of sports in which institutionalized violence occurs, such as American football or boxing. Serious fan violence affects the socio-emotional feelings of winning by tarnishing the joy, almost euphoria, of an important and often exciting victory. If some fans commit vandalism or attack police or other emergency service personnel, then the important victory is less pleasing and joyful and becomes a source of embarrassment and sadness. Thus, psychological harm may be created by serious fan violence.

Sport serves a *socialization* mechanism by teaching and reinforcing the basic values of society, such as being rewarded for success in competition or hard work. Socialization through sport is challenged by serious fan violence. What the violent celebrating fan is saying, in effect, is "I can be antisocial through violence by showing my happiness for my team's success." Often, after an act of fan violence has occurred, we see fans pointing their index fingers in the air and shouting, "We are number one." The violence clearly challenges widespread notions of what appropriate fan behavior should be after major victories.

The *integrative* function of sport describes how sport serves to tie significant groups together in communities, such as Ohio State football fans or Red Sox baseball fans. In some cases the integrative function can go beyond groups to societies, such as countries that are supporting their World Cup soccer team or countries following their athletes in the Olympics. The integrative function of sport is harmed by celebrating fan violence because the violent fans are in essence saying, "We have a way to celebrate that the other fans cannot participate in after a major victory." The violent celebrating fan creates a community independent of all the other communities associated with the victory. These other communities (for example, older fans, women) want to celebrate an important victory of their team, but in ways that are socially acceptable. Hence, the violent fan becomes estranged from the general community of fans, thus reducing the integrative impact of sport.

The *political* function of sport serves to promote the prevailing ideologies of society. For example, sport promotes the values of following rules and accepting punishment when the rules are not followed. An example would be the yellow and red cards in soccer. The political function of sport suggests that sport facilitates the general development of ideological systems in society. The argument is that ideology is important for the normal functioning of society. Serious fan violence attacks the idea that society has an orderly pattern to it, that is, that society can develop and change in systematic ways. Celebrating fan violence, as well as other types of fan violence, introduces, however briefly, a great deal of randomness into the system.

Lastly, sport serves as a source of *social mobility* in society. It has been argued than many football players could not have gone to college because of costs if they had not received football scholarships. Thus, the social mobility function refers primarily to the athlete. If fan violence harms the victory, then it is possible that the athletes taking part in the game will also be harmed, in the sense that their financial viability will be reduced. While there is no empirical evidence to support this, the theoretical possibility remains.

Serious Fan Violence as Pollution

Now that I have looked at the structure of sport and serious fan violence, this question should be asked: How does a society respond to this harm? This analysis views serious celebrating fan violence as a social crisis which is conceptualized as social pollution. Three ideas guide this discussion. First, major sporting events such as championship play become defined as *sacred* and highly valued because of their functional contributions to society or significant groups within society. Second, these social events become damaged, or *polluted*, by the introduction of tragic elements such as serious fan violence. Third, society mitigates the impact of the pollution by reacting through the use of sacred, or "religious," and secular rituals. Several writers have provided insight into aspects of this adaptation process. I begin the discussion by looking at sport as a sacred phenomenon.

A basic assumption of this book is that organized sport, whether collegiate or professional, plays a very important part in society. Sport can be viewed, as I noted, as having an integrative function, assisting in creating solidarity in the group and fostering a feeling of belonging to a certain group. Because of the solidarity-creating functions of sport, it can been seen as having "sacred" qualities, fulfilling religious functions.

The events of competitive team sport become highly valued, particularly major championships. The sacred aspects of sport have been described in an analysis by Nixon and Frey (1996, 64), where they link seventeen characteristics that are present in both sport and religion. Some of the more important traits are the "quest for perfection, asceticism, intense feelings and claims of special virtue." All these values are supported by sport and religious rituals. From a European perspective, Coles (1975, passim) proposes that both sport and religious rites reflect a type of social process at work which supports the feeling of the group. Referring to sport as a "surrogate religion," Coles suggests that both sports activities and prayers should be considered an experience which focuses on feelings of the sacred and emphasizes a social significance attached to such an occasion. He observes that sporting occasions and places associated with them may possess considerable significance for players and spectators. Coles views religion as multidimensional, social, and identified according to the feelings it arouses, which feelings are then expressed and amplified in social contexts.

The second idea is the potential for harm that sports fan violence can cause. Major sporting contests, particularly championship play—such as the Super Bowl in professional football, the Final Four in men and women's collegiate basketball, the Frozen Four in professional hockey, and World Series in professional baseball—have the potential for the introduction of tragic events, particularly with serious celebrating fan violence. When this happens, the unique nature of the event is profaned by the pollution of the tragedy.

The third set of ideas involves society's response to the pollution. For theoretical insights into society's response, I now turn to Jeffrey Alexander's model.

Ritual Reactions to Sports Tragedies

The analysis of ritual reactions to serious celebrating fan violence is guided by models developed by Alexander (1988) and Lewis and Veneman (1987). These events, or reactions, are examined to show how society adapts to the social crisis. In particular, the rituals of purification include public statements, visits and pilgrimages, official inquiries, services and memorials, and fund-raising organizations. Through the public expression of grief, anger, and sadness, there occurs a collective process of cleansing the society of the pollution caused by injuries or deaths of the fans and an expression of support for the central values of society.

Jeffrey Alexander's work on ritual and the Watergate crisis builds on the scholarship of Emile Durkheim and Mary Douglas. Durkheim (1965) theorized that religious rituals were culturally defined social patterns which assisted in maintaining integration and stability in society. Rituals and the public expression of religious fervor are identified as social functions which were enacted to strengthen bonds in the social system. Rituals recognize the power of disorder, that is, pollution in the system. Following a sporting disaster, the social value of the event is polluted and can have no place in society until purified or renewed. For example, following the Hillsborough disaster in England where many soccer fans were killed, other football clubs and supporters were unwilling to go ahead with scheduled games and dedicated the canceled games as a mark of respect to the Hillsborough victims.

Mary Douglas (1966) built on Durkheim's work by specifying the social nature of profane acts. Douglas suggests that a sacred ritual or symbol is polluted (hence, profaned) when a tragic and unexpected element is introduced. I argue that important football matches in England are examples of highly valued social events that take on sacred dimensions that can be polluted.

Jeffrey Alexander (1988) formulated hypotheses to examine adaptation to a social crisis. Michael Veneman, Anne Marie Scarisbrick-Hauser, and I, using modifications of the Alexander model, analyzed the ritual responses to two English soccer tragedies, the Bradford fire (Lewis and Veneman 1987) and the Hillsborough crowd crush (Scarisbrick-Hauser and Lewis 1990).

The Alexander model is based on the premise that any society responds to any crisis in predictable ways. Alexander studied a political crisis, the Watergate scandal. In June 1972, some employees of the Republican Party broke into and burglarized the Democratic Party headquarters in the Watergate Hotel in Washington, DC. Two years later, the Watergate incident had become the catalyst for a serious political crisis in American society. The Watergate crisis polarized society into sacred and profane elements of society and created the need for some kind of ritual cleansing and renewal of the political arena to enable a return to routine life (Alexander 1988).

The Bradford fire and the Hillsborough tragedy generated ritual responses with participants from every walk of life. Lewis and Veneman (1987) and Scarisbrick-Hauser and Lewis (1990) noted that ritual responses come from the secular community, including senior political officials, sports officials, local community leaders, and the sacred community characterized by national religious leaders and local religious leaders. The processes of response included public statements, memorial services, visits to the sites, officials investigations, and fund-raising. The following propositions, while based on deaths associated with a terrible fire and a crowd crush, can be applied to serious fan violence.

Theoretical Propostitions

The following propositions derived from the previously discussed essays are used to explain the ritual reactions to serious sports fan violence, particularly celebrating riots, in North America.

1. Serious fan violence is seen as having a harmful effect on North American society.
2. Serious fan violence is viewed as detrimental to spectator sports.
3. Serious fan violence stimulates a variety of ritual reactions that contribute to the purification of spectator sport.

Analysis

Proposition 1: Harmful Effect

Serious sports fan violence has a harmful effect on society. To examine this pattern of harm, I begin with the Ohio State riot analyzed in chapter 6.

Ohio State Riot

Major sports championships receive wide coverage from television, radio, and the press. Typically at major championship events there are experienced television and radio crews covering a game; the presence and commentary of top sports professionals give the fan violence situation a sense of solemn occasion and sadness. Often reports of celebrating fan violence begin to appear soon after the game has finished. This happened at the Ohio State riot when Ohio State beat Michigan. The field invasion was shown to the nation on television. The television viewers of a nationally broadcast game saw the attack on police and the goalposts as the game between Ohio State and Michigan ended.

The harmful effect on society is illustrated in these reactions to the Ohio State riot. Turnbull, Gebolys, and Thomas write, "For many at the university and its alumni, as well as central Ohioans, the news reports brought shame. An incensed Mayor Michael B. Coleman [of Columbus] raged about the destruction of his city by out-of-control kids. An embarrassed OSU President, whom some had rebuked for earlier comments about the rude fan behavior, apologized on behalf of the Ohio State University community" (2002, 2). A citizen of Columbus wrote this about the Ohio State University and the riots: "Several of us residents care deeply for the university as an important institution of higher learning. . . . But, we are losing the battle, especially every time these riots occur" (Pfau 2002, 7A).

Note that the story is presented with a tone of shame and embarrassment, suggesting that the celebrating fan violence can cause pollution in this form as least, for central Ohio as well as for Ohio State University Buckeye fans. However, the pollution may have an even wider scope. For example, the same news story quotes the talk show host Jay Leno as joking that the first responsibility of the new Department of Homeland Security was "to protect Americans against Ohio State football fans" (Turnbull, Gebolys, and Thomas 2002, 1A).

Proposition 2: Detrimental Aspects

Not only are the events of serious fan violence viewed as harmful to society, they are generally viewed as detrimental to the particular sport involved as well as spectator sports in general. This proposition deals with the issue of "threat to the 'core' values" of the sport noted at the beginning of this chapter and is seen as a social crisis.

The sacred space, the sports playing field, has been polluted. The importance and symbolism of the occasion increased the sense of pollution: a "sacred" ritual had been damaged. It was as if the members had been killed in their church. There is something unnerving about going out to a sports arena for a relaxing evening in a safe environment and ending up having to fight for your life.

The *Lantern*, the Ohio State University student newspaper, wrote, editorially, that "In one night, a group of Buckeye fans took matters into their own hands and managed to tarnish the victory the football players had worked so hard for. The players earned their win with class, and the so-called 'fans' couldn't let them enjoy their sweet success" (*Lantern* 2002, Opinion section). Clearly again it is possible to see the language of pollution with ideas of "tarnish" and "sweet success."

The Red Sox Riot

The Red Sox riot was also seen as harming both society and baseball (Propositions 1 and 2). In this case "society" may be seen as the wider community of Boston, Massachusetts, as well as greater New England. Indeed, Red Sox fans in these areas refer to themselves as being part of "Red Sox Nation." This is one of the few teams in major league baseball that has a collective term used to represent this body of fans. Others might be "Die Hard Cub

Fans" for the Chicago team or "The Bums" for the old Brooklyn Dodgers. The importance of the American League Championship Series (ALCS) victory and the subsequent World Series Championship was summed up by the FenwayNation.com (2004) blog: "The 2004 Red Sox have given the Nation what legions of fans have sought so desperately for generations—redemption. Finally, the taunting ends, the chants stop, the curses are forever stilled."

The pollution of society and baseball happened in two ways. First, the death of Ms. Snelgrove, along with the injuries and arrests, greatly tarnished the ALCS victory and continued to do so even after the Red Sox had won the World Series. Both of these victories were enormous successes for the Red Sox team and Red Sox Nation. John Henry, the Red Sox owner, said, "The victory [in the ALCS] was the greatest comeback in baseball history." Yet, the tragedy of the riot destroyed the joy of success. Trot Nixon, a Red Sox player, said about Ms Snelgrove, "I'd give back Game 7 to have her back" (Hohler 2004).

Second, the rioting was harmful to society and baseball, particularly baseball, because it occurred near the sacred site of Red Sox baseball: Fenway Park. Fenway Park is one of the oldest professional baseball sites in the Major Leagues. It has a storied history. Babe Ruth pitched Fenway, Mickey Mantle and Roger Maris of the Yankees hit back-to-back home runs in the park, and Ted Williams hit his last home run there (Updike 1960).

Within the sacred space of Fenway Park, there is an even more sacred section: the "Green Monster," or the left-field wall of Fenway. Much of the riot action took place when the Boston police came into conflict with male fans who were trying to climb the Green Monster from the street in an attempt to get access to the field. A few officers began firing at the climbers, who then retreated. Shortly after this occurred, Ms. Snelgrave, who was standing a few yards from the Green Monster wearing a Red Sox sweatshirt, was killed.

Proposition 3: Ritual Reactions

When serious fan violence occurs, ritual processes that contribute to the purification of sport come into play. This is the most important process in the Lewis and Veneman (1987) model. Social rituals are used to repair and purify both the society and sport. Through a series of ritual events, the damaged or profaned social system is declared ready to resume normal life. The processes that society is involved in include public statements and prayers, visits to the site, memorials, governmental inquiries, and fund-raising campaigns. Let's look at each of these in turn in relation to the Ohio State and the Red Sox riots.

Public Statements and Prayers

Many public statements are issued within hours of serious fan violence, often by the president of a university or the general manager of a professional team. Typically these statements say that the fans causing the problem were not the "true" fans of the team. The prevailing response to the Ohio State riots was shame. The *Columbus Dispatch* noted that celebrating riots "would become an embarrassment that drew national attention to a city and school celebrating a hard-fought victory." In the same story, Karen Holbrook, the president of Ohio State University, apologized for the rude fan behavior, "on behalf of the Ohio State University community" (Turnbull, Gebolys, and Thomas 2002, 1–2).

After the Red Sox riot in Boston, the public statements began almost immediately, with the prevailing response primarily being a sense of tragedy. Perhaps the most poignant was Snelgrove's father, Rick, who met reporters outside his home, with a picture of Victoria, saying, "I want you to meet my daughter" (Porter 2004, 1).

Kathleen O'Toole, the Boston police commissioner, said that "the Boston Police Department is devastated by this tragedy. This terrible event should never have happened" (*CNN.com* 2004).

Memorial and Religious Services

Serious fan violence can be responded to with memorials, religious ceremonies, and services, particularly if a death occurs.

There is no evidence that there were any memorial or religious services held in response to the Ohio State riots.

However, in regard to the Red Sox riot there were several memorial services for Ms. Snelgrove. Three stand out. Five hundred mourners attended her funeral at St John's Catholic Church in East Bridgewater, Massachusetts, including the governor of Massachusetts and the mayor and police commissioner of Boston. The pastor who gave the eulogy blamed the rioting fans for the tragedy (Lavoie 2004).

A few days later, just before the start of first game of the World Series, there was a moment of silence while Ms. Snelgrove's name and picture were put on the giant screen in the center field of Fenway Park. Interestingly this moment of silence came before the national anthem was played. Lastly, a year after her death, a memorial service was held in the Journalism Department of Emerson College where she attended.

Visits and Pilgrimages

When serious fan violence occurs, the site of the violence takes on an identity which can be defined either as a place to visit or to make a pilgrimage. A visit is less emotionally intense than a pilgrimage. A visit is an information-seeking activity. A pilgrimage involves a desire to go to the place and join in the religious experience present in the area. Often the site is decorated with floral tributes and statements of regret and remembering.

In the absence of photographic evidence and other reports, it is only possible to speculate about the visits to the sites of the Ohio State riots. However, it seems quite likely that some students and others did go to the riot area simply to look at the damage: the burned-out automobiles and damaged store fronts.

The sites around Fenway Park lent themselves to memorials and pilgrimages, but there is little empirical evidence that this occurred, other than one story on the placing of flowers at the site where Ms. Snelgrove died. However, I think it is safe to suggest that the site took on a sacred quality with people visiting it since it is readily accessible from Kenmore Square. Indeed, I visited the site in the spring of 2005.

Official Investigations

When serious fan violence occurs, generally there will be official investigations. In the case of collegiate fan violence, the universities involved often establish a committee to study the event and issue a report of its findings. In addition, the local police agencies will generally look into the incidents and sometimes issue a report. Depending on the seriousness of the violence, local newspapers will generally do extensive analyses of the events and often publish site maps showing the location of fan violence.

Ohio State University's response to the rioting was to appoint the Task Force on Preventing Celebratory Riots. This task force was created jointly by Karen Holbrook, the president of Ohio State University, and Michael Coleman, the mayor of Columbus, Ohio, in early December 2002 and was chaired by David Andrews, the dean of the College of Human Ecology. It issued its *Final Report* (Task Force 2003) on April 7, 2003 (see appendix B). There were two sets of recommendations. One set called for the entire community to work together to creative a more positive approach to the enjoyment of an important collegiate sports victory. The other set proposed thirteen specific recommendations for "minimizing the likelihood of riots in the near future" (Task Force 2003, 2). For example, one specific recommendation called for letters to parents of students spelling out the consequences of alcohol violations and riot behavior (Task Force 2003, 16).

The press also investigated the riots. Two papers are important to this analysis. The major paper of Columbus is the *Columbus Dispatch*, and the major student paper is the *Lantern*. For over two weeks, these papers regularly published articles and photographs about the celebratory rioting, which provided a very useful body of information about the events.

In regard to the Red Sox riot, there were major investigations into the riot with most centering on the death of Ms. Snelgrove. One was by the Suffolk district attorney with an eye toward prosecution. Another was an internal investigation by the Boston Police Department. Eventually the officer in charge of policing during the celebrating riot retired, although he claimed that it was not because of the Snelgrove tragedy.

However, the most important investigation was done by the Stern Commission appointed by Boston police commissioner Kathleen O'Toole. The commission, headed by Daniel K. Stern, a well-known Boston lawyer and professor at the Harvard Law School, issued a report entitled *Commission Investigating the Death of Victoria Snelgrove*. The report was relatively narrow in its focus, looking at the circumstances of Ms Snelgrove's death and the use of the FN303 weapon, a projectile propelling weapon used for crowd control. In summary, the Stern report said that (1) the Boston Police Department had intelligence that there would be a large crowd celebrating the victory if it occurred; (2) there was poor communication between police officers and commanders during the riot; and (3) the officer should not have fired at Ms. Snelgrove because she was moving and was in the middle of the crowd. The most serious criticism was directed at the Boston Police Department for its training and improper use of the FN303 weapon. It is clear that the Stern Commission had Ms. Snelgrove's tragic death in mind as it did its work. In the preface the commission comments, "Finally we should not forget a person who is always in our thoughts. . . .Torie [as she was known] was a wonderful and caring person. . . . We hope that the lessons learned as a result of this tragic death will guide law enforcement agencies, so similar tragedies will not occur" (Stern Commission 2005, iv).

Fund-Raising

Often after serious fan violence fund-raising activities begin, typically involving media organizations, sports figures, and popular culture personalities such as rock stars or movie actors and actresses. The monies raised generally go to pay medical or funeral expenses or to the development of memorials for the dead. These fund-raising activities contribute to the ritual of purification by attempting to show the tragedy of the fan violence and its causes. By identifying the causes, the pollution can be eliminated as elements within society work to solve the causes of the fan violence associated with a particular sporting disaster.

There is no evidence of any public fund-raising associated with either the Ohio State or Red Sox riots, as had been the case in previous crowd tragedies. However, there was a money dimension that can be seen as a response to the pollution of the Red Sox riot. In May of 2005, the city of Boston announced a settlement with the Snelgrove family. It included five million dollars, a scholarship fund, and a public memorial. The five millions dollars was paid in the form of a three-million dollar cash settlement and a two-million dollar annuity. A spokesperson for the Snelgrove family said that the scholarship was seen as a memorial to Victoria (Stack 2005).

Summary and Conclusions

This analysis has suggested that serious fan violence, particularly celebrating violence, has a very negative effect on sport and that a society tends to respond to this pollution with a series of ritual responses to resolve the pollution and return sport back to an equilibrium. In the Ohio State situation the primary response to the pollution was collective shame and embarrassment, while with the Red Sox rioting the response was sadness, primarily because of the death of Victoria Snelgrove, and the tainting of the victory over the Yankees.

The rituals of responding to the societal crisis of pollution differ from one crisis to another. The findings of this chapter suggest that, in at least two cases, social crises resulting from the celebrating rioting were so serious that some type of symbolic closure and purification of pollution was needed.

I have noted the consequences of serious celebrating fan violence and the responses to it. In the next chapter I examine the solutions that have been proposed to combat this violence.

References

Alexander, J. C. 1988. "Watergate and Durkheimian Sociology." In *Durkheimian Sociology: Cultural Studies*, ed. J. Alexander, 187–224. Cambridge: Cambridge University Press.

CNN.com. 2004. "Boston Police Accept 'Full Responsibility' in Death of Red Sox Fan." October 22. www.cnn.com/2004/US/10/22/fan.death.

Coakley, J., and E. Dunning, eds. 2000. *Handbook of Sports Studies*. London: Sage Publications.

Coles, R. 1975. "Football as a Surrogate Religion?" In *Sociological Yearbook of Religion in Britain*, ed. Michael Hill, vol. 8, 61–77. London: SCM Press.

Douglas, M. 1966. *Purity and Danger: An Analysis of Concepts of Pollution and Taboo*. London: Routledge & Kegan Paul.

Durkheim, E. 1965. *The Elementary Forms of the Religious Life*. Trans. Joseph Ward Swain. New York: The Free Press. (Orig. pub. 1915.)

FenwayNation.com. 2004. "Thank you, 2004 Red Sox." fenwaynation .com.

Hohler, B. 2004. "Pesky Happy to Be Back." www.boston.com.

Lantern. 2002. "Riot's Aftermath." December 9, opinion section.

Lavoie, D. 2004. "Hundreds Mourn Loss of Student Killed by Police during Red Sox Celebrations." *USA Today*, October 26. www.usatoday/ sports/baseball/al/redsox/2004-10-26-fan-funeral_x.htm.

Lewis, J. M., and M. J. Veneman. 1987. "Crisis Resolution: The Bradford Fire and English Society." *Sociological Focus* 20 (2): 155–68.

Loy, J. W., and D. Booth. 2000. "Functionalism, Sport and Society." In Coakley and Dunning 2000, 8–27.

Nixon, H. L., and J. H. Frey. 1996. *A Sociology of Sport*. Belmont, CA: Wadsworth Publishing.

Pfau, E. L. 2002. "Lack of Respect on Game Days Could Kill Neighborhood." *The Columbus Dispatch*, December 14, 7A. www.dispatch.com.

Porter, T. 2004. "First Draft"/"Apologize For What." October 22.

Scarisbrick-Hauser, A. M., and J. M. Lewis. 1990. "Theoretical Approaches to Societal Reactions to the Hillsborough Soccer Disaster." American Sociological Association annual meetings, Washington, DC.

Stack, D. 2005. "Snelgroves Weigh Suit against Gunmaker." *boston.com*, May 3. www.boston.com.

Stern Commission. 2005. *Commission Investigating the Death of Victoria Snelgrove*. Boston: The Boston Police Department.

Task Force on Preventing Celebratory Riots (Task Force). 2003. *Final Report*. Columbus: The Ohio State University.

Turnbull, L., D. Gebolys, and A. Thomas. 2002. "Reconstructing the Riot: What Happened . . . and What Didn't." *The Columbus Dispatch*, December 8, www.dispatch.com.

Updike, J. 1960. "Hub Fans Bid Kid Adieu." *New Yorker*, October 22. Reprinted in the *Boston Globe*, July 7, 2002, C5.

8

Solutions to the Problems of Fan Violence

In this chapter I will examine a variety of solutions that have been proposed to solve the problem of fan violence in North America. These include reduced availability of alcohol to potential rioters, increased police presence, moral persuasion by coaches and athletes, more accurate coverage by the mass media, and scholarly research. I begin the discussion by looking at the issue of the approval of fan violence.

The Approval of Fan Violence

The question of the public approval of fan violence has been largely ignored by researchers. That scholars have not looked at the phenomenon of the "boys will be boys" attitude toward sports riots may be due to the fact that this form of collective violence is often thought to be nonpolitical, and hence approval or disapproval is essentially nonpolitical as well. There are two problems that need to be studied in regard to approval of fan violence: first, the approval or disapproval of sports riots by the general public, and second, the approval of riots by the official agencies of the society—particularly the police.

There seems to be tacit approval of fan violence by Americans. This is particularly true for college students in regard to riots of celebration, which are generally defined as nonpolitical (see chapter 4). James Michener (1971), in his book on Kent State, noted that the riots after the 1970 Michigan–Ohio State football game caused more damage and involved more people in Columbus, Ohio, than the riot leading up to the shootings at Kent State. Michener (1971, 461) notes, "The Ohio State riot was conducted by persons who adhered to the older life style; . . . it was recognized as a part of our traditional heritage. We knew how to handle it, how to jolly it along."

The interpretation of civil disturbances is essentially a public opinion process (Lewis 1982b, passim). To understand this process for fan violence, and particularly celebrating riots, draws on the theoretical insights provided by Ralph Turner (1969) in his essay, "The Public Perception of Protest." Turner argues that publics assign meaning to disorders. He writes, "We assume that individuals and groups of individuals assign simplifying meaning to events, and then adjust their perceptions of detail to these comprehensive interpretations" (Turner 1969, 817). Turner suggests that the interpretation of racial or student collective violence ranges along a continuum from criminal rioting to social protest. He sees at least five different perspectives that one can use to interpret whether a civil disturbance will be defined by publics as social protest or criminal rioting (Turner 1969, 817–18).

First, publics test events for credibility in relation to folk conceptions of social protest and justice. Second, disturbances communicate some combination of appeal and threat, and the balance is important in determining whether the disturbances are regarded as social protest. Third, disturbances instigate conflict with a target group, who may define them as social protest in the course of attempted conciliation to avoid full-scale conflict. Fourth, defining disturbances as protest is an invitation for a third party for the troublemaking group to form a coalition. And fifth, acting as if the disturbances were social protest can be a step by public officials in establishing a bargaining relationship.

Turner's first point on the credibility of violence is very important to the understanding of collective violence of sports fans, and it is necessary to present his views on this issue in more detail. Turner (1969, 818) thinks that for civil disturbances to be defined as protest, they must "somehow look and sound like social protest to the people witnessing it." Thus, argues Turner, people and events involved in collective violence must be seen as credible before the violence will be deemed social protest as opposed to criminal rioting. These propositions are suggested by his essay:

1. Civil disturbances are defined as social protest only when they fit a folk concept of social protest. Turner thinks that members of American society have developed a conventional wisdom about collective violence. This conventional wisdom, or folk concept, is used to decide whether the collective violence of a civil disturbance is a social protest or criminal rioting. He writes, "To be credible as protestors, troublemakers must seem to constitute a major part of a group whose grievances are already well documented, who are believed to be individually or collectively powerless to correct their grievances, and show some signs of moral virtue that render them 'deserving.' Any indication that only a few participated or felt sympathy with the disturbances predisposes observers to see the activities as deviance or as revolutionary activity by a small cadre of agitators" (Turner 1969, 818).

2. Civil disturbances are defined as social protest by those groups who see themselves as more advanced than those who participate in the disturbance. If a group is perceived as "truly" disadvantaged, then their actions seem to be more credible. Thus, Blacks using violence as social protest are seen as more reasonable than "advantaged" college students.

3. Civil disturbances are more likely to be defined as protest by social classes that hold a consensual view of society based on common values than by those social classes that do not hold such views. Turner (1969, 820) writes, "When judgments by different socioeconomic strata are compared, the middle strata find it more difficult to credit massive deviance and crime and less difficult to acknowledge protest because of their commitment to

society as a system of values. The lower strata have more day-to-day experience of crime and the rejection of societal values, and are forced to anchor their security to a less consensual image of society. Hence, they do not find massive crime so difficult to believe."

It is possible to use these ideas when dealing with the public evaluation of collective violence and sport. Smelser's strain position (1962) would see fan violence as a form of social protest against underlying social problems not necessarily related to the sport. In contrast, Marx's issueless riot approach (1970) would likely place the violence in the criminal rioting category.

The insights from Turner (1969), Smelser (1962), and Marx (1970) suggest that the interpretation of sports riots as social protest or issueless riots is determined by two factors: (1) the situational context in which the riot occurs and (2) the social position of the person who interprets the riot.

Essential to Turner's argument is the idea that people make judgments about the appropriateness or lack of appropriateness of civil disturbances in the situational context in which they occur. When Turner (1969) asserts that collective violence can be deemed credible as social protest, he is, in fact, describing a more general notion that people attempt to make sense of civil disorders in terms of their views of the situational context in which the violence takes place.

The Official Approval of Fan Violence

The official agencies that deal with fan violence are the local police and related groups like the state police and National Guard. As noted in earlier chapters, the action of the police can have a devastating effect on a crowd. Marx (1970) argues that a crowd that sees itself as celebrating can become political and guided by hostile beliefs if members of the crowd deem the action of the police to be inappropriate. No doubt there are many factors that go into the police's definition of a sports riot's course. These factors include their evaluation of the general public approval or disapproval of the riot; whether the riot is believed to be clearly linked to the sporting event per se or to more diffuse causes; and whether there is a tradition of rioting vis-à-vis the particular sport or event.

Solutions for the Problem of Sports Fan Violence

Moving away from the issue of public approval, I turn to several solutions that have been proposed to eliminate or reduce the problem of celebrating fan violence. The solutions include alcohol reduction, increased police presence, statements by coaches and athletes, more accurate coverage by the mass media, and scholarly research. I have tried to present both the positive and negative aspects of these solutions. The positive would be the reduction of sports fan violence, while the negative would be the unanticipated consequences of these solutions, such as increased violence. In any case, this chapter is designed to stimulate discussion of issues related to preventing fan violence, including raising ethical issues about the control of fan violence.

Alcohol Reduction

At first blush the thought that reducing or eliminating alcohol would result in the elimination of celebrating fan violence is very attractive: a simple solution to a complex problem. The argument, often put forward by police and city officials, goes something like this: Celebrants of a major sports victory have been drinking heavily during the championship event. When the championship concludes, the winning team's fans move to a natural urban gathering place, where, because of reduced inhibitions and a lack of social control, they become violent. Solution—eliminate the booze.

There are several problems with this solution. First, it is difficult to limit access to alcohol because in most situations the individuals doing the drinking are either doing so in private residences or in public bars and restaurants where the drinking age rules do not apply or are easily subverted. Alcohol is a high-profit area for sport, therefore bar owners would be reluctant to eliminate this source of income.

Second, there are some assumptions about alcohol and violence that need to be evaluated. It is not always correct to assume that there is a direct correlation between extensive drinking and street violence. For example, Clark McPhail, in a private communication, notes that many street festivals, such as Oktoberfests, have large amounts of alcohol consumption and there is very little violence associated with the events. The same can be said about Mardi Gras celebrations.

A question can be asked: How good are people in making judgments about alcohol and rioting? One possible theoretical approach to this questions is called social norming (Berkowitz 2004, 5). Social norming is defined as the condition where an individual's behavior is influenced by incorrect perceptions of how other members of a group think and act. According to Berkowitz (2004, 7), social norming takes three forms—pluralistic ignorance, false consensus, and false uniqueness. Pluralistic ignorance occurs when "a majority of individuals falsely assume that most their peers think differently from them when in fact their attitudes and behavior are similar." False consensus is the false belief that others are like one's self, and false uniqueness is "when individuals in the minority assume that there is a great difference between themselves and others." The primary misconception of the violent fan is that his peers will approve of acts of serious violence. Indeed, during crowd actions, it is possible to watch violent fans seeking approval of spectators. But, in fact, most peers disapprove of serious violence such as attacking police officers, firemen, and women and other EMS (emergency medical service) personnel, as was shown in chapter 4. Thus, fans willing to commit serious violence are social norming using the mechanism of false consensus by believing that other celebrating fans are equally willing to be violent for purpose of recognizing and honoring an important sports victory.

There is some empirical evidence that is useful in helping us determine the relationship between drinking and celebrating sports among college students. An Ohio State University study conducted in 2001 using a random sample of undergraduates found that 28 percent of the sample thought that "Party goers drinking too much" was a major cause of campus rioting in

Columbus, Ohio (Office of Student Affairs Assessment 2001). Turning to NCAA Division I basketball, Kaplowitz and Campo (2004) found in a survey (N = 1992–1997) conducted after the 1999 Final Four riot at Michigan State that 19 percent of the students strongly disagreed or disagreed with the statement "The University is trying to control student drinking too much," while 64 percent agreed or strongly agreed with the statement (Kaplowitz and Campo 2004, 506). These data suggest that alcohol is seen as a cause of a rioting by about one-third of all students. Or, in other words, students look for other explanations for the rioting that go beyond the simple explanation of too much drinking.

Thombs, Olds, and Snyder (2003), at Kent State University, did a field study of blood alcohol concentration (BAC) of college students (N = 1020) and found those with a low BAC overestimated their level of intoxication, while student with a high BAC underestimated their intoxication. While the authors did not examine issues of violence, this study seems to suggest that linking fan violence to alcohol, particularly in terms of self-reports and the claim "I was drunk" as an explanation for violence, needs to be called into question. The writers found that estimated BAC explained only 20 percent of the variance of actual BAC.

This discussion suggests that we cannot automatically link celebrating fan violence to drinking. Yet, it is clear that drinking is present when celebrating fan violence occurs. My view is that drinking gives the violent fan permission to do what he wanted to do anyway. Because the celebrating fan is highly pleased with his team's victory, he wants to do an act that celebrates the victory and can be linked to the sport. Thus, he commits vandalism, throws missiles, sets fires, or fights with social-control forces, seeing these acts as feats of skill akin to the acts that take place on the playing field. The violent fan seeks permission to do this. Some of this comes from the support of fellow celebrants. Closely linked to the idea of a fan violence support structure is the issue of alcohol consumption. Does drinking allow the violent fan to disavow his violence by letting him blame the violence on too much alcohol consumption? McCaghy (1968) found this pattern of deviance disavowal among child molesters, and it might be a factor in the support structure of violent fans. The tendency to attribute one's violence to excessive drinking may also be another aspect of the "boys will be boys" belief system. This is particularly true for low-level violence.

Lastly, the English experience with soccer hooliganism supports the argument that alcohol is not a major explanatory factor in fan violence. The leading scholars on British hooliganism write, "Drinking, for example, cannot be said to be a significant or 'deep' cause of football hooliganism for the simple reason that not every fan who drinks, even heavily, takes part in hooligan acts. Nor does every hooligan drink, though a stress, not only on fighting but also on heavy drinking, is integrally involved in the masculinity norms that are expressed in their behavior" (Dunning, Murphy, and Williams 1986, 225).

The Role of Police and Security Forces

Another solution that is often proposed to deal with celebrating fan violence is increased police presence along with more aggressive policing. No doubt there are many factors that go into the police's definition of fan violence. These factors include the police's evaluation of the general public approval or disapproval of the riot; questions of whether the riot is believed to be clearly linked to the sporting event per se or to more diffuse causes; and whether there is a tradition of rioting vis-à-vis the particular sport or specific event.

Police and security forces have a difficult time with fan violence. The approval study that began this chapter shows that there is considerable public support for low levels of fan violence. Thus, many police agencies respond to potential violence by creating an arena for the violence. For example, it is my impression that this is what takes place at the Ohio State–Michigan football game in Columbus, Ohio. An arena for celebration is created on High Street, the main street in Columbus, where fans congregate after a game. However, if fans do not follow the "rules," then the police are likely to react with violence, particularly if the spectators carry out their celebration at inappropriate places. This practice of "arena creating" by police has the potential of becoming out of hand, encouraging the police and fans to react to each other with increased violence. I showed this in chapter 6 in reference to the Red Sox riot, where the arena-creating pattern did get out of hand in Boston.

Second, there is another problem with aggressive policing. The police actually harm the people they are trying to control. This is what happened in Boston in 2004 as noted in chapter 6. The research of Adamek and Lewis (1973) two years after the Kent State University shootings by the Ohio National Guard showed that excessive social-control violence has a radicalizing effect on demonstrators, and they become more aggressive in later crowd actions. Too aggressive policing clearly can result in long-term harm to the fans and the sport in general or, in Kent State's case, loss of life and long-term harm to representatives of the university as well as social-control forces.

The third problem with policing is the frequent reluctance by police to get involved in large-scale crowd control activities. There are three reasons for this. First, crowd control is very difficult and unpredictable before, during, or after sporting events, particularly when there is crowd violence because of the emergent qualities of crowds. One is never sure of what is going to happen. Police officers are trained in protocols which often do not apply to unruly sports crowds. Second, such arrests generally do not hold up in court. What a violent fan looks like when he is arrested is generally not what he looks like when he shows up in court, although this is also true of the burglar and drunk driver. Lastly, the families of police officers do not like them getting involved in crowd control. Often spouses or significant others of police officers discourage them from taking crowd-management assignments for fear of possible injuries or entangling court appearances.

An alternative to social control by police only is the use of the student and faculty marshals. One alternative that warrants consideration is the use of unarmed peace marshals for crowd control, particularly on college campuses. Such personnel have been effectively used in civil rights and student protests. Marshals who are peers of the violent fans could create situations where rapport could be readily established, hence reducing or eliminating fan violence and its support structure. Peers could do this because they are more likely to understand the culture of the violent fan better than the police (Lewis 1982a). The aforementioned Ohio State study found that 76 percent of students said that students should be the "most responsible to stop rioting" (Office of Student Affairs Assessment 2001, 5).

Over the years, I have trained student and faculty marshals (D. Lewis nd) in conflict resolution on campuses. I think that a program of student and faculty marshals would be useful in keeping sports celebrating activities peaceful on campus. My approach to marshaling has as its roots in three philosophical and empirical areas. The philosophical background for the training is based on the thought of Gandhi, while the empirical sources are organized around the analytical work of Clark McPhail (see chapter 2) and my own research on techniques of crowd control used by English police at football (soccer) matches (Lewis 1982c).

I begin the training with ideas from Gandhi with this thought (Merton 1964, 24): "There is no half way between truth and non-violence on the one hand and untruth and violence on the other. We may never be strong enough to be entirely nonviolent in thought, word, and deed. But, we must keep nonviolence as our goal and make steady progress toward it." With these ideas and others, I try to get students and faculty to understand three basic points: First, being nonviolent is not something that is automatic, but rather something that has to be worked at in a very conscious manner. Second, one can use values and feelings of nonviolence to tap into the goodness and willingness of others to be nonviolent. Third, someone who is working in a conflict resolution program needs to be introspective about his or her own potential to be violent and must learn to manage these attitudes and feelings.

The second underpinning of the marshaling training comes from Clark McPhail. As noted in chapter 2, he has developed a series of categories that allow the observer to understand what is going on in a crowd. I try to teach students and faculty that crowds have texts that can be read and understood in the same way that one would read the text of a poem or a film. The categories allow the observer, particularly when one combines categories, to understand the dynamics of crowds, including celebrating sports crowds. For example, a typical crowd might be chanting, surging, and gesturing about an exciting, important sports victory. This event can quickly be interpreted using McPhail's categories. It is possible to interpret what is going on, at a particular time, by using these and other of the McPhail categories. What I try to develop in marshals is a sense of crowd literacy so they can be more comfortable in their conflict resolution efforts.

The last source of background for the training comes from my own empirical research on how English police control crowds in an essentially nonviolent manner. There are many ideas that are used in the training, but the most important is teamwork. I stress in the training that marshals should always work in teams of two to four people. This provides several things to the team members: encouragement for their work; knowledge, in the sense that someone in the team will know what to do; and more effective reduction of potential violence, because research has shown that people working together have a better chance of reducing someone's violence than if one is alone. The training should always include simulation of mock violence as well as the noise of the celebrating sports crowd. I believe college and university administrators should consider the use of the student and faculty marshals as a resource in preventing violence after important sporting event victories.

One major objection to the use of marshals is that crowds do not want to be controlled and are not capable of pro-social behavior. Let me illustrate my point with three stories—one from the Bible, the second from the "sixties," and the third from empirical research.

My favorite biblical story is the feeding of the five thousand by Jesus with five loaves of bread and two fish. If we assume this was a "miracle," then the story is over. But, if we assume it is crowd behavior, then we have a different situation. Can you imagine a man coming to his wife and saying, "Let's go to the desert and listen to this preacher from Nazareth?" What would a good Jewish mother and wife do? She would pack a lunch. The crowd seeing and listening to the goodness of Jesus begins to share their lunches with each other because of the rituals of a positive religious experience.

Some years ago during a discussion of rock concert violence in my class on collective behavior, one of my students reported the following incident at a concert in Detroit: A small fire began on the stage, and there was movement toward the exits. The folk singer said, "Be calm, let your brothers and sisters live." It worked and there was an orderly exit. Jesus's actions as well as the folk singer's words tapped into the social structures and cultures of the crowd resulting in pro-social behavior.

However, we can go beyond the Bible or the "sixties" for examples of pro-social activities. The work of Norris Johnson (1987) and Johnston and Johnson (1988) from the University of Cincinnati are two sources. They examined secondary data on crowd situations involving panic or potential panic conditions at a fire and at a rock concert. With regard to The Who concert where a crush happened, Johnson's research showed that 75 percent of those interviewed reported some type of helping behavior, including giving, receiving, or observing help. Forty percent of those interviewed reported help in all three categories (Johnson 1987). At the Beverly Hills Supper Club fire in Kentucky, 58 percent of the employee sample reported giving some kind of help, including directing people to exits, reporting the fire, and fighting it (Johnston and Johnson 1988). Scholars of sports riots need to explore questions associated with pro-social behavior and celebrating sports riots.

Athletes and Coaches: Their Responsibility

There are significant others, in addition to peers, who might contribute to the reduction of celebrating fan violence. The two groups that are the most important are athletes and coaches.

Teams and sponsor schools should use the media to have athletes speak to fans about respectable behavior. Athletes can take a greater responsibility in crowd control. I do not mean just during or after the game, but rather in setting the tone prior to the event. I think the athlete has the obligation to communicate to the fans that appropriate team support does not involve screaming insults, disrupting a game, tearing up stadia, or fighting with fellow fans or with players. Neil Offen (1974), in *God Save the Players*, writes that there is an ambivalent attitude toward fan violence: "This kind of violence, seen on the front pages and in the living rooms, creates an extremely difficult situation for team owners, managers and officials. If all this beer-throwing and fighting is going on in their stands, it appears that they are running a shabby operation. It looks like they should have put their money into hiring enough uniformed guards instead of into the new, exploding, contracting, living, breathing scoreboard." But more importantly, the public violence forces the teams to make an ethical choice. Can they discourage beer throwing and fighting when they've spent all this time and all this promotion money to encourage rabid fanaticism? They have urged their fans to become involved, to care, and what are they to do when the fans become a little too involved, or care too ardently? Thus, the courageous athlete, when he speaks against fan violence, may be going against the wishes of his own team.

Well-known coaches also can play a role in preventing fan violence, by suggesting ways to properly celebrate a victory and again, using the media from student newspapers to national television to get the message out. Recently Big Ten coaches such as Joe Paterno of Penn State and Jim Tressel of Ohio State have been making statements in television public service announcements encouraging student football fans to celebrate in appropriate ways.

The National Mass Media and Fan Violence

The mass media have raised the issue of American fan violence as a serious social problem. This is commendable. However, there are still problems with the manner in which the media present the violence.

First, the media tend to report incidents of fan violence in rather vague terms. Participants are referred to as fans, bums, rioters, thugs, and so forth. It would be more appropriate to describe those involved in more precise demographic terms of gender, race, age, and whatever additional indicators are available. Second, the media need to be more precise in their reporting of the actual behavior involved. The typology of behavior suggested previously throughout the chapters may be useful in such a presentation. Third, the media need to deal more precisely with the actual role of alcohol in the violence. Newspaper reporters need to determine, to the best of their ability, the extent that violent fans and their supporters have been drinking. Fourth, newspaper reporters need to separate, in terms of their analysis of fan violence, those who are actually violent from those who are acting in verbal support of the violence and those who are simply observers. For example, some newspaper accounts of the baseball Cleveland beer riot in 1974 left the impression that over twenty thousand people were involved when, in fact, no more than one thousand were involved, and for most of the time, far fewer than that number actually participated.

Scholarly Research

The data presented in the previous chapters indicate that fan violence is a social problem in the United States. It is surprising that sociologists have not devoted much attention to this phenomenon, but there are three reasons for this. First, sociologists have not been interested in the sociology of sport as a legitimate research area, although Luschen (1980), in his review of the literature, indicates that the sociology of sport began in the 1950s (except for a few publications around the turn of the century) and became a subfield of general sociology in the 1960s. The second reason is that there are not many sociologists doing work in crowd behavior (Quarantelli and Weller 1974). Further, most collective behavior scholars working on riots in the last decade have been concentrating on crowd behavior related to either the civil rights movement or student unrest and antiwar crowd behavior. Thus, the skills and interests of sociologists have not been directed toward problems of recreational and sports riots. A third reason is the fact that research on fan violence may be dangerous. Berk (1972) has discussed the problem of danger in the study of crowds, and his conclusions are clearly applicable to the study of fan violence.[1]

The time has come for sociologists and other students of collective violence to recognize the topic of fan violence as a valid research topic. In the pages that follow, I will present several research questions that the scholarly community should address.

Newspapers will probably continue as a major source of data because of the difficulty involved in actually anticipating an incident of fan violence, particularly with the development of the LexisNexis archive. However, Danzger warns us that there can be biases built into the data because of the fact that most conflict data are reported by the wire services (United Press International, Associated Press). He adds, "Reports of the occurrence of an event and many elements of the description, such as the number and type of participants, the actions occurring and so forth may be accepted as fact. Given the structure of corrective processes, such facts are more likely to be valid if gathered for a time sequence rather than for a single event" (Danzger 1975, 581).

An important question is, How serious has the fan violence been? A way to approach this issue is by using indices of fan violence. A very useful study tool is J. Wanderer's (1969) Index of Riot Severity. The application of this scale to fan violence is straightforward. The intensity of the riot is conceived as a combination of the variable number of participants, duration of the outburst in terms of the amount of continuous days, and number of separate sites within a city where the protest simultaneously occurred.

The Wanderer's scale is scored as follows:

	Items	*Points*
Duration:	one day	1
	two days	2
	three or more days	3
Sites:	one site	1
	two sites	2
	three or more sites	3
Participants:	5–75	1
	76–200	2
	201+	3

The lowest possible score is three and the highest is nine.

Appendix A presents the most serious sports riots for universities and professional sports in North America since 1960. Using these data and the Wanderer index might be a good way to continue research on sports fan violence. I would like to suggest some hypotheses that combine the ideas of comparing university and professional sports riot severity.

> *Hypothesis 1.* The severity of fan violence varies directly with the importance in the status of the competition (e.g., playoff game, championship game versus a regular season game).
>
> *Hypothesis 2.* University sports crowds generate more severe fan violence than do professional sports crowds.
>
> *Hypothesis 3.* There is a direct relationship between the violence of sport per se and the severity of fan violence.

Most of the research on fan violence has examined the structural characteristics of individuals and situations. Thus, we know that fan violence is mostly carried out by young, white males at championship-related games and matches. This is certainly a useful beginning, but it is not the best way to expand a body of knowledge about fan violence. A better way to continue fan violence research is to direct attention toward (1) relationships among rioters and (2) interaction between rioters and the social control forces.

To guide the inquiry in this area, the work of Clark McPhail discussed in chapter 2 is valuable. In an earlier article McPhail argued that attitudes and demographic variables are not very predictive of who participates in crowd actions. He writes, "Civil disorders are complex and differentiated phenomena. Attempts to account for their occurrences and individual participation therein have failed to acknowledge this complexity, theoretically and operationally. This shortcoming has been magnified by focusing on the 'status' or attributes of communities and individuals as causal variables" (McPhail 1971, 1070).

What is the implication of McPhail's ideas for the study of fan violence? Basically, it is this: In researching causes of fan violence, it is essential for scholars to look at relationships among sports crowd members. One way to begin to look at fan relationships is in terms of their attitudes and behavior about winning and losing (Ball 1976). In the United States celebrating violence tends to be carried out by fans of the winning team, particularly after championship games. However, in England the violence is often punishment directed at the winning team's fans by the fans of the losing team. In the States, the violence is usually vandalism or fights with the police, while in England the violence usually involves fighting or missile throwing between two groups of fans, each supporting a different team.

A second issue of crowd relationships deals with friendship patterns and the makeup of crowds. It seems reasonable that sports crowds are made up of small groups of individuals who know each other. For example, Aveni (1977, 98) found that 74 percent of the people in a precrowd assembling pattern after an Ohio State–Michigan football game were with at least one other person. It may be that violent fans are supported by others in groups of twos and threes.

A third research issue is the soccer (football) fan violence, which is the greatest venue for fan violence worldwide. Soccer is a rapidly growing American professional sport. The North America Soccer League (NASL) was formed in 1968. From 1968 to 1975, the league experienced great financial difficulties, with many of the franchises exchanging owners and home cities. Growth was slow as the paying public was not easily attracted to soccer as a major sport in America. Eventually, however, the marketing and exposure of soccer did catch up to the expectations of NASL and its financial backers—mainly due to the formation of numerous youth leagues and the signing in 1975 of Pelé from Brazil, the greatest player in soccer history. Over the next two years, Pelé and the NASL doubled their average game attendance and some teams averaged over thirty-five thousand fans a match. In 1977, Pelé's last season in America as a player, seventy-seven thousand people watched the New York Cosmos team in a play-off game with the Fort Lauderdale Strikers. However, the NASL failed and ceased operations in 1984.

What is the potential for fan violence in soccer in North America? In late 1993, Major League Soccer was formed and began play in 1996. During the years 1996–2004 average attendance ranged from 15,559 to 17,406 ("Major League Soccer" 2005). However, some writers think that interest in professional soccer will continue to grow. One reason is that the United States team qualified for the World Cup in 2006 in Germany, although it did not do very well in the competition. Another is the growing number of young people playing soccer in the United States. According to American Sports Data (2005), soccer participation has increased 88 percent from 1990–1991 to 2002–2003. It is estimated that about 47 percent of all high school players are girls.

There has really been no serious fan violence at American professional soccer matches. I believe this is due, at least in part, to the demographics of U.S. soccer crowds, which are likely made up of a higher percentage of women as well as fans who have attended college and have higher than average incomes.

Another possible explanation for the absence of violence is the lack of intense identification by the fans with the teams and players. Of course, it may only be a matter of time before the young teams obtain a loyalist following that may be prone to the type of violence evident in American football, baseball, and basketball. American soccer should be placed in a crosscultural context. One way is to look at how different societies determine what constitutes "fan problems." For example, an insult in England is two fingers raised in a reverse "peace sign." I have seen fans ejected from a soccer match for doing this. In the United States that gesture would mean nothing. Differing policing techniques can give us some insights into how societies view fan behavior. I (Lewis 1982c) found that in England police can engage crowds much more directly than is possible in the United States.

Conclusion

Each of these recommendations for solving the problem of fan violence in North America requires analysis and debate. This debate should begin in the host community of the sport—the college or university, in the case of collegiate sports, and the city in professional sports. I believe the potential for a serious episode of fan violence is present wherever fans gather to watch a sports event. Consequently, the debate on a social policy to control spectator violence should be given immediate attention by responsible members of the sporting community. Appendix B reports the recommendations of the Ohio State University short- and long-term policies for dealing with celebrating riots. These are a good starting point for leader discussions on dealing with the problem of fan violence, not only at colleges and universities, but in cities as well.

To die or be seriously injured by fan violence is like a plot in an Albert Camus novel. To be killed in a sports riot as the result of action from fellow rioters or the social-control forces is utterly tragic. Perhaps research into the various phenomena described in this book might prevent someone from losing his or her life in such an event. To write about a single public policy for fan violence suggests too narrow an approach because the violence affects and can be affected by many segments of society: the scholarly community, the mass media, the athletes, the police, and violent fans themselves.

Note

1. In 1988, I was in the Old Town area of Dusseldof studying the behavior of fans during the European Championship soccer matches when I found myself caught between German and English fans who were fighting each other. As I dove into a doorway to avoid the missiles, I wondered if I was in the right line of work.

References

Adamek, R. J., and J. M. Lewis. 1973. "Social Control Violence and Radicalization: The Kent State Case." *Social Forces* 51(3): 342–47.

American Sports Data. 2005. "Soccer Voted Hottest Sport in the U.S." www.americansportsdata.com/index.htm.

Aveni, A. F. 1977. "The Not-so-Lonely Crowd: Friendships Groups in Collective Behavior." *Sociometry* 40 (1): 96–99.

Ball, D. W. 1976. "Failure in Sport." *American Sociological Review*. 41 (4): 726–39.

Berk, R. A. 1972. "The Controversy Surrounding Analyses of Collective Violence." In *Collective Violence*, ed. J. F. Short Jr. and M. E. Wolfgang, 112–18. Chicago: Adline.

Berkowitz, A. D. 2004. "The Social Norms Approach: Theory, Research, and Annotated Bibliography." Ms (alan@fltg.net, www.alanberkowitz .com).

Danzger, H. M. 1975. "Validating Conflict Data." *American Sociological Review*. 40 (5): 570–84.

Dunning, E., P. Murphy, and J. Williams. 1986. "Spectator Violence at Football Matches: Towards a Sociological Explanation." *British Journal of Sociology* 37, no. 2 (June): 221–44.

Johnson, N. R. 1987. "Panic and the Breakdown of Social Order, Popular Myth, Social Theory." *Sociological Focus* 20: 171–83.

Johnston, D. M., and N. R. Johnson. 1988. "Role Extension in Disaster: Employee Behavior at the Beverly Hills Supper Club Fire." *Sociological Focus* 22 (1): 39–51.

Kaplowitz, S. A., and S. Campo. 2004. "Drinking, Alcohol Policy, and Attitudes Toward a Campus Riot." *Journal of College Student Development* 45, no. 5 (September/October): 501–16.

Lewis, D. Nd. "Data Sources and the Study of Rock Crowds." Unpublished manuscript, Kent State University, Kent, OH.

Lewis, J. M. 1982a. "Peacemarshalling." *Peace and Change* 8, nos. 2–3 (Summer): 73–80.

Lewis, J. M. 1982b. "Fan Violence: An American Social Problem." In *Research in Social Problems and Public Policy*, ed. M. Lewis, 175–206. Greenwich, CT: JAI Press.

Lewis, J. M. 1982c. "Crowd Control at English Football Matches." *Sociological Focus* 15, no. 4 (October): 417–27.

Luschen, G. 1980. "Sociology of Sport: Development, Present State, and Prospects." *Annual Review of Sociology* 6: 315–47.

"Major League Soccer." 2005. *Wikipedia*. http://en.wikipedia.org/ wiki/Major_League_Soccer.

Marx. Gary T. 1970. "Issueless Riots." *Annals* 391 (September): 21–33.

McCaghy, C. H. 1968. "Drinking and Deviance Disavowal: The Case of Child Molesters." *Social Problems* 16 (l): 43–49.

McPhail, C. 1971. "Civil Disorder Participation: A Critical Examination of Recent Research." *American Sociological Review* 36 (December): 1058–73.

Merton, T., ed. 1964. *Gandhi on Non-Violence*. New York: New Directions.

Michener, J. 1971. *Kent State: What Happened and Why.* New York: Random House.

Montreal Star. March 18, 1955.

Offen N. 1974. *God Save the Players: The Funny, Crazy, Sometimes Violent World of Sports Fans.* Chicago: Playboy Press.

Office of Student Affairs Assessment. 2001. "OSU Student Involvement in and Opinions about the Off-Campus Disturbances." The Ohio State University: Office of Student Affairs Assessment, 1–8.

Quarantelli, E. L., and J. M. Weller. 1974. "The Structural Problem of a Sociological Specialty: Collective Behavior's Lack of a Critical Mass." *American Sociologist* 9 (May): 59–68.

Smelser, N. J. 1962. *Theory of Collective Behavior.* New York: The Free Press.

Thombs, D. L., R. S. Olds, and M. Snyder. 2003. "Field Assessment of BAC Data to Study Late Night College Drinking." *Journal of Alcohol Studies* (May): 322–30.

Turner, R. H. 1969. "The Public Perception of Protest." *American Sociological Review* 34 (December): 815–31.

Wanderer, J. 1969. "An Index of Riot Severity and Some Correlates." *American Journal of Sociology* 74 (March): 500–505.

Appendix A

Serious Celebrating Fan Violence Linked to Collegiate and Professional Team Championships in the United States, 1960–2004

This appendix reports data on serious celebrating fan violence associated with championships for the four major team sports of football, baseball, basketball, and hockey in the United States. The incident is initiated and carried by fans of the winning team. A serious incident of celebrating fan violence is defined as an event that has one of the following criteria: one or more deaths, five or more injuries, or ten or more arrests. Reported crowd size or damages were not used as they are considered relatively unstable and inadequate measures of crowd structures. From 1960 to 2004, using newspaper data, I identified fifty-five incidents of fan violence associated with championship play. Twenty-three of these crowd incidents met one or more of the criteria for being a serious riot. Table A.1 lists the ten most serious riots associated with professional team sports, while table A.2 lists the five most serious for collegiate team sports. The listings are from the most recent event to the earliest.

Table A.1 Ten Most Serious Celebrating Riots (CR) Associated with Professional Team Sports, 1960–2004[a] (most recent to earliest)

Date	Venue	Sport	Narrative	Source
October 2004	Boston	Baseball	A celebrating riot (CR) after Red Sox beat the Yankees. One person killed, six injured, six arrested.	Boston Globe (see chapter 5)
June 1996	Chicago	Basketball	CR following Bulls' victory, in the NBA championship. Thirty-eight stores looted, 656 arrested.	New York Daily News
June 1993	Chicago	Basketball	CR after Bulls' victory in NBA championships. Three people killed, one hundred officers injured, 682 arrested.	Associated Press
February 1993	Dallas	Football	CR after Cowboys won Super Bowl. Fourteen injured, twenty-four arrested.	Chicago Sun-Times
June 1991	Chicago	Basketball	CR after Bulls victory in NBA championships. One hundred arrested.	South Bend Tribune
June 1990	Detroit	Basketball	CR after Pistons won NBA title. Seven deaths, hundreds injured, 141 arrested.	Boston Globe
October 1984	Detroit	Baseball	CR after Tigers won the World Series. Many injured, 34 arrests.	Chicago Tribune
January 1975	Pittsburgh	Football	CR after Steelers won Super Bowl. Scores of injuries, 233 arrested.	Cleveland Plain Dealer
October 1971	Pittsburgh	Baseball	CR after Pirates won World Series. Many rapes, fifty persons injured.	Boston Globe
October 1968	Detroit	Baseball	CR after Tigers won World Series. One rape and one hundred arrested.	Washington Post

Table A.2 Five Most Serious Celebrating Riots Associated with Collegiate Team Sports, 1960–2004[a] (most recent to earliest)

Date	Venue	Sport	Narrative	Source
November 2002	Columbus	Football	CR (celebrating riot) after Ohio State beat Michigan for Big Ten title. Fifty-eight to seventy arrested.	*Columbus Dispatch* (see chapter 5)
April 2002	Minneapolis	Hockey	CR after Minnesota won NCAA title. Six police injured, twenty-four arrested.	*San Antonio Express*
April 2002	College Park	Basketball	CR after Maryland won NCAA title. One officer injured, seventeen arrested.	Associated Press
March 1974	North Carolina	Basketball	CR after NC State won tournament game. Three to five officers injured, thirty-one arrested.	*Cleveland Plain Dealer*
November 1970	Columbus	Football	CR after Ohio State beat Michigan. One rape, three officers injured, forty-five injured.	*Akron Beacon Journal*

[a]Tables A.1 and A.2 are modeled on a table format developed by Kevin Young, "Sport and Violence," in *Handbook of Sport Studies*, ed. J. Coakley and E. Dunning (London: Sage Publications, 2000), chap. 25, 384.

Appendix B

Recommendations of the Ohio State University Task Force on Preventing Celebratory Riots

Campaign Goals

The goals for this campaign will be to:

A. *Instill pride and enhance the positive engagement of students in both their university and their community.* This will be evidenced by mutual respect, proactive involvement, and a sense of ownership of university and community issues.

B. *Promote safety and health within the student body.* This will be evidenced by healthy decisions related to alcohol and drug use, reduced incidents of unsafe activities, and increased involvement in health-promoting activities.

C. *Prevent illegal and irresponsible behavior within the student body.* This will be evidenced by lower rates of behavior requiring disciplinary action, fewer illegal acts in the University District and in the larger community, and fewer incidences of irresponsible behavior.

Campaign Recommendations by Goal

Goal A: Instill Pride and Enhance Positive Engagement

1. Form an association of major owners and managers of rental property in the University District to provide a forum for addressing community issues. Explore mechanisms for student involvement in these discussions. The university's Office of Student Affairs and these property owners and managers should cooperate in the utilization of Ohio State's student judicial system to respond to violations of the Code of Student Conduct in private rental housing in the University District. These owners and managers also should agree on lease provisions that will reduce unlawful behavior, alcohol consumption, and out-of-control parties and will improve the physical environment. The lease provisions could include prohibition of or limits on kegs of beer; prohibition of indoor furniture used on porches; limits on density; prohibition of items in inappropriate areas, such as furniture or barbecue grills on roofs. Consider adopting the model used in East Lansing, Michigan, where rental property owners employ private security to police properties and ensure compliance with code and lease terms.

2. The university and city should investigate innovative approaches, such as social norms marketing, to communicate positive messages to students, other members of the university community, and visitors. Communications and public education strategies should involve "peer-to-peer" communication, should use humor, and should have an interactive component. The communication and public education campaigns must be evaluated carefully for their effectiveness. The focus of this campaign should be broader than violence reduction and should include fan behavior, civility, and mutual respect.

3. Encourage neighborhood pride among students through increased service-learning and volunteer projects. Such efforts should target residence hall students, as well as those that live in the neighborhood.

4. Make selected improvements to the public right-of-way that will enhance the image of the University District. Specifically, sidewalk improvements, street trees, and lighting upgrades should be implemented. Improvements to refuse collection and a prohibition on indoor, stuffed furniture placed on outdoor porches should be pursued.

5. The Office of Student Affairs should explore establishing its living-learning centers in the student neighborhoods, as well as on the university campus. These facilities offer a sense of performance and stability currently lacking in the neighborhood. Facilities could be staffed with university personnel and may house students who would live in the area for longer than just one year.

6. The university should consider purchasing a few selected, strategic problem properties that contribute to density or public safety difficulties within the student neighborhood.

7. The university and the city should establish a goal of attracting a larger percentage of more mature residents as a stabilizing influence in and around the student neighborhood.

8. The university should expand its Faculty-Staff Neighborhood Homeownership Incentive Program with a special emphasis on homeownership opportunities in or adjacent to the student neighborhood. The university should consider a substantial increase in the incentive to promote homeownership in targeted areas. The city should consider targeting its homeownership programs to opportunities in the University District.

9. The Office of Student Affairs and area property owners and managers should explore strategies for establishing positions similar to a resident manager or resident advisor in the student neighborhood. The persons in these positions could provide a sense of stability, a source of information, and a means of communication among the students, other neighborhood residents, property owners, property managers, the university, and the city. The university's new Community Ambassador Program, which is being funded by several major property owners, is in its

pilot phase this year. This program, if successful, could be expanded and meet this need. Another approach would be for property owners and managers to hire resident managers.

Goal B: Promote Safety and Health

10. Increase the number of activities that help engage students in both university and community life. These activities should include but not be limited to, late night activities developed at alternatives to alcohol consumption. Creating large-scale activities that attract students is challenging and requires substantial investment and student involvement in design and implementation. It should be noted that the purpose of activities is to engage students at all times, not just to provide a substitute to participating in riots.

11. In cooperation with area property owners and managers, the University Area Review Board and the city should consider measures to deal with the public safety problems posed by second-story party decks, and, if necessary, they should consider a grant program or other incentive to remove the decks.

12. During game days, Lane Avenue has increasingly developed an "anything goes" celebratory culture that many believe sets the stage by appearing to condone if not to encourage high-risk drinking and antisocial behavior. Modifying this culture should be part of long-term implementation strategies. Specific recommendations of the Task Force include:

- Keep private tailgating parties in designated areas and regulate alcohol-related behavior.
- Eliminate or severely restrict street vendors on Lane Avenue on game day to allow for better regulation of sidewalk and street behavior.
- Request that radio stations and other media sponsoring the parties along Lane Avenue contribute finan-

cially and/or in kind to the communications and public education campaigns regarding high-risk drinking and acceptable fan behavior.

13. Concerted and well-integrated efforts should be made to stigmatize high-risk drinking and to promote student health and safety through:

- Increased information at orientation to students and their parents regarding high-risk drinking.
- Required substance abuse sessions for all incoming students, including an individualized approach that employs motivational interviewing.
- Use of class projects in areas such as media, marketing, cultural, and public health to advance the prevention agenda.
- Support of responsible drinking programs such as designated driver, safe rides, regulated tailgate on south campus, and student organizations like BACCHUS and GAMMA.
- Involvement of high-visibility athletes and "star" faculty in encouraging a message of safe partying.
- Consistent delivery of the message that Ohio State University is a non-party school of parents, faculty, staff, alumni, and more, through such routes as recruiters, admissions, and orientation.
- Use of the stadium screen for public service announcements on social norming related to alcohol consumption.

Goal C: Prevent Illegal and Irresponsible Behavior

14. The university and the Columbus police should develop a student-police community relations group to discuss relevant issues of student safety and student-police relations. This group would be an extension of the existing community relations officer program sponsored by the Columbus police, but its focus would be on providing a venue specifically for students to interact with police on

a regular basis. The goal for the group would be to develop an increased sense of community in the student residential neighborhoods and to foster improved relations between the student residents and the officers who service those neighborhoods.

15. Representatives of the university and the city should respond to speculation about potential riots with a low-key, but consistent, message that illegal behavior will not be tolerated in any neighborhood, including the University District. The goal is to reduce media speculation about riotous behavior, which, at least in part, becomes a self-fulfilling prophecy.

16. Strictly enforce safety, fire, occupancy, criminal, building zoning, and health codes, including density and green space provision for the University District; simultaneously correct any weak, vague, or inadequate codes.

17. Costs associated with disturbances should be calculated and broadly communicated. These include costs of police, fire, clean-up, university staff, and programming, as well as costs to victims, community members, and the reputation of the institution.

18. The university and city should work with Lane Avenue business owners on joint policing and liquor control efforts.

19. Owners of rental property in the student neighborhood should redevelop a portion of their units with a market orientation toward graduate and graduate-age professional students, recent graduates, and other young professionals.

20. The university should conduct research regarding prevention and intervention activities that discourage and stigmatize antisocial riot behavior and that can be utilized by local law enforcement with student crowds.

21. The university should continually evaluate any new activities, policies, and practices to determine effectiveness with a commitment to discontinue any approaches that are ineffective.

22. The university should continue to evaluate the effectiveness of alternative activities in reducing riots and illegal and high-risk drinking.

SOURCE: Task Force on Preventing Celebratory Rioting, *Final Report* (Columbus: The Ohio State University, 2003), 10–14.

Appendix C

A Value-Added Analysis of the Heysel Stadium Soccer Riot

On May 29, 1985, a riot occurred at the European Cup Final soccer championship between Liverpool and Juventus at Heysel Stadium in Brussels, Belgium. The riot, which caused the death of thirty-nine soccer fans, had a profound effect on English society as well as on professional soccer. This essay uses Smelser's (1962) general model of collective behavior to analyze data derived from a number of sources describing the Heysel Stadium riot. In particular, this analysis focuses on a period of four hours, from the beginning of the riot at about 7:30 p.m. until the conclusion of the match around 11:30 p.m.

On May 29, 1985,[1] a riot occurred at the European Cup Final soccer championship between Liverpool and Juventus at Heysel Stadium[2] in Brussels, Belgium. The riot, which caused the death of thirty-nine soccer fans, had a profound effect both on English society as well as on professional soccer. The next day headlines all over the world announced the terrible news. Americans

Original article: J. M. Lewis, "A Value-Added Analysis of the Heysel Stadium Soccer Riot," *Current Psychology* 8, no. 1 (1989), 15–29. Reprinted with the permission of Transaction Periodicals Consortium, Rutgers University.

learned of the riot from television and newspapers. For example, *The New York Times* (5/30/85, p. 1): "Riot in Brussels at Soccer Match Leaves 40 (sic) Dead."

This essay uses Neil J. Smelser's (1962) general model of collective behavior to analyze data derived from a number of primary and secondary sources describing the Heysel Stadium riot. In particular this analysis focuses on a period of time of four hours, from the beginning of the riot at about 7:30 p.m. until the conclusion of the match around 11:30 p.m.

Before looking at the soccer riot, it seems appropriate that we examine its consequences. Obviously, the deaths and injuries at Heysel were the most serious consequences of the riot. But, there were others. English national pride was damaged. The queen of England wrote to the president of Italy saying, "I am deeply saddened that so many lives were lost . . ." (*The Daily Telegraph*, 5/31/85, p. 2). She also sent a statement of regret to King Baudouin of the Belgians saying, "I was very shocked by the terrible events in Brussels . . ." (*The Daily Telegraph*, 5/31/85, p. 2). Prime Minister Margaret Thatcher wrote to the prime ministers of Italy and Belgium expressing sympathy and revulsion over the events at Heysel and announcing that the government would contribute 250,000 pounds to a disaster fund for the families of the victims (*The Daily Telegraph*, 5/31/85, p. 2).

English soccer was under attack after Heysel. Almost immediately after the riot all English football league clubs were banned from playing in Europe and elsewhere. Gradually, a few of the restrictions were lifted, and by the Fall of 1985, English clubs were allowed to play exhibitions in Europe but not in major cup competitions. Moreover, Liverpool, a major soccer power in England and Europe, was banned from European Cup competitions for an indefinite time. The ban on all cups competition was enforced through 1988. The English national team was banned for a short time, but did return to play in the 1985–1986 season.

The Belgian government came under severe attack for its handling of the riot as well as the subsequent investigation into it. The prime minister offered his resignation to the king, but it was refused. However, the riot did contribute to the eventual fall of the government. In January, 1987, Albert Roosens, the Belgian Soccer Union secretary general, was charged with involuntary manslaughter through negligence (Cleveland *Plain Dealer*, 1/28/87, p. 4-E). In the United States, this would be the equivalent of the commissioner of baseball being indicted for a riot at Fenway Park. In addition, two gendarmerie officers were indicted. Finally, twenty-six Liverpool fans were indicted for various crimes associated with Heysel and were scheduled for trial in the Fall of 1988.

Theoretical Considerations

Smelser's model of collective behavior sets forth a set of concepts and propositions which can be used to order all variations in collective behavior. The five determinants of collective behavior are labeled structural conduciveness, structural strain, growth of a generalized hostile belief, mobilization of participants for action, operation of social control. Lewis (1982a) has suggested that to adequately apply Smelser's model, one must use the subdeterminants to the model as well.

Structural Conduciveness

The first necessary condition is called structural conduciveness and refers to situations generated by the social structure that provide a range of possibilities within which a hostile outburst can occur. This determinant can be understood in terms of the variables, (a) the structure of responsibility, (b) the presence or absence of channels for expressing grievances, and (c) the facilitation of communication among the aggrieved. In relation to a sports riot, it becomes necessary to determine, for example, whether fans believe that someone is responsible for the failure of their team to win or if their team is being insulted. This responsibility might include players, coaches, referees or other fans. Further, it should be determined if the fans think there are channels for expressing their grievances. Lastly, the analyst must decide if fans are able to communicate with each other.

Structural Strain

This determinant describes conditions of strain that fall within the components of conduciveness. The strain is particularly at the level of norms and values in crowd situations. Strain is in itself not enough to cause an outburst. Rather, it contributes its "value" to the eventual outcome if an outburst does occur. The strain determinant requires that the investigator determine if a sports riot is tied into a more general community problem and not related specifically to a particular sporting episode.

Growth of a Generalized Hostile Belief

In all episodes of collective behavior, including sports riots, beliefs prepare participants for the ensuing action. A belief spreads through the action of the precipitating factors. In addition, the precipitating factors can have certain specific effects in supporting the general conditions of conduciveness, strain, and spread of the hostile belief. The notion of the generalized belief is a key variable in Smelser's formulation. In regard to a sports riot, it requires that one locate a set of beliefs or attitudes that have served to direct the behavior of the sports fans.

Mobilization of Participants for Action

The final stage of the value-added process in a hostile outburst is the actual mobilization and organization of action. The spread of a hostile outburst falls into two categories. Smelser (1962, p. 259) says that any hostile outburst can be looked at as having a real and derived phase. The real or initial phase results from the build-up of conditions prior to the beginning of the outburst. In the derived phase, however, the hostility may become unrelated to the conditions giving rise to the initial outburst. The question for the analyst is whether a sports riot begins for reasons related to more general social conditions of the game per se and shifts for reasons related to social control. For example, the police actions may become the focal point of the riot if they use force deemed inappropriate by the rioters.

The Control of Hostile Outbursts

This is more of a counter-determinant. The exercise of norms can be in the form of a counter-determinant of a preventive sort (dealing with conduciveness and strain), such as sporting norms which discourage the use of fan violence as part of the sport. Social control force, or the threat of force, can also be a counter-determinant which deters the sports riot if properly exercised or increases the riot's severity if perceived to be improperly applied.

The implication of Smelser's model for sports riot research is that any explanation of such a riot should be based on variables which explain the riot as a hostile expression of underlying strains and grievances.

Data Sources

This study is a case history. An enormous amount of material has been generated over the Heysel Stadium riot because of the loss of life as well as the consequences of the riot for British and European politics and soccer. My sources include print and electronic media, the Popplewell Report (1985, 1986), a site visit to Heysel Stadium and discussions about Heysel with students at the Catholic University of Leuven where I spent the spring semester of 1988 as a visiting professor.

Print media sources include a systematic study of *The Times* (London) from the first issue after the hostile outburst through the April 30, 1988 issue and *The Manchester Guardian Weekly* from June 2, 1985 through December 8, 1985. In addition, I drew on articles and photographs from other English newspapers. I used photographs from the French publication *Match* (Paris) which show the consequences of the riot.

I studied photographs from seven Belgium newspapers that were published on the day after the match and used translations of the two major Belgium papers, *De Standaard* and *Le Soir*.[3]

From the American press, I reviewed a variety of sources including *Sports Illustrated, Newsweek, Time,* the *New York Times* and other periodicals. By far the most helpful was an essay by Clive

Gammon (1985) in *Sports Illustrated*. Gammon's article is a model of good sports writing about riots.

I drew on electronic media primarily through audio tapes made by an English friend, Ian Maclean, of interviews conducted on English radio and television with eyewitnesses, scholars and officials. In addition, I screened a tape which shows part of the riot and its aftermath that is available at the Communication Department of the Catholic University of Leuven.

The Popplewell Reports (1985, 1986) were issued in two parts. They are based on an investigation of the Heysel incident by Lord Popplewell, a senior English judge. He and his staff studied various aspects of Heysel, as well as the Bradford Fire, and the reports are good sources of information about the physical aspects of the riot.

On February 24, 1988, I visited Heysel Stadium in the company of two policemen who had been present when the Heysel riot happened. During this visit I spent considerable time studying the physical aspects of the terraces where the riot occurred. I also had an interview with a leading authority on soccer hooliganism in Belgium, Kris Van Limburgen, a member of the staff of the Catholic University of Leuven. Lastly, it should be noted that I have done field work on European soccer in England (Lewis, 1982b).

Narrative: Heysel Stadium, May 29, 1985

The European Cup is one of the major soccer events of the year. It involves league champions from two different countries who have made it through an international competition to play for the cup. The final match is always played in a third country as a neutral site for the game. The match was scheduled to begin at 8:15 p.m. on Wednesday, May 29, 1985, at Heysel Stadium in Brussels, Belgium.

Typically, a soccer ground opens two hours before kickoff, but often fans gather in the town near the stadium, singing and chanting in preparation for the match. These gatherings, often accompanied by drinking, can begin as early as four hours before the match, but usually happen in the afternoon or early evening of match day.

There is evidence according to Gammon (1985, p. 24) that Liverpool fans were arriving as early at 7 a.m., more than twelve hours before the match, at the Belgium port cities of Zeebrugge and Ostende. In the afternoon of match day, many Liverpool fans moved into Brussels' squares with the ever-present public urination and litter which is typical of large English soccer crowds. In midafternoon, a Liverpool supporter was stabbed (not seriously) by a Juventus fan (Gammon, 1985, p. 24). Later, the Popplewell Report notes, more trouble was caused by Juventus fans in Heysel when they began fighting with police (Popplewell, 1986, p. 6). This happened at the opposite end of the stadium from where the major riot took place.

In the late afternoon, supporters of both teams began moving toward Heysel Stadium. As fans entered the stadium, there was some yelling back and forth between X and Y and Juventus in Section Z. The taunting was strongest among fans closer to the thin fence separating the two sections. Typical insults from an English point of view, are such things as using the reverse peace sign which is the equivalent to the raised middle finger in the United States; or calling opponents or their supporters "wankers" which means that they are so weak and effeminate that all they can do is masturbate. There were some bottles and fireworks thrown, and possibly concrete pieces.

About 7:20 p.m., 55 minutes before the start of the match, a small number of Liverpool fans initiated two charges against Juventus supporters, using long flagstaffs and metal bars broken from a thin fence that had been separating the two groups (Gammon, 1985, p. 25). After these two shoving and pushing episodes, a strong surge by the Liverpool fans occurred at 7:29 p.m. The Juventus supporters near the fence attempted to get out of the way. This led to the second part of the crowd action—a crush. Gammon writes (1985, p. 25);

> One eyewitness described the Italian section as 'a swirling river of bodies' cascading downward. Within minutes, hundreds of fans found themselves at the bottom of section Z,

crushed by more and more bodies behind them and cornered between a six-foot-high chain-link fence that fronted the field and a two-foot thick concrete wall that formed one end of the standing room area. Almost simultaneously, the fence and wall collapsed, pitching hundreds of pressing fans into a hideous pileup in which those at the bottom were trampled and pinned under bodies and debris.

The immediate consequence of the hostile outburst and crush which lasted about six and one-half minutes was the death of 38 fans, including thirty-one Italians, four Belgians, two Frenchmen and one Britain. Most died from suffocation. In addition there were over 400 injured. Later, a Sicilian, who had been in a coma, died from his injuries.

In about one and a half hours the police restored order and the match was played. Juventus won 1–0 on a penalty kick.

Analysis of the Heysel Stadium Riot

This analysis used Smelser's model, both determinants and subdeterminants, to order and explain the data about the Heysel riot. The analysis begins with structural conduciveness.

Structural Conduciveness

What conditions were generated by the social structure that facilitated the hostile outburst? Smelser proposed that the analyst look at three subdeterminants, which he describes as: the structure of responsibility, the presence or absence of channels of communication, communication among the aggrieved.

The Structure of Responsibility

A crowd that is carrying out a hostile outburst is usefully divided into social roles. One system of roles proposed by Lewis (1972) sees a crowd as made of an active core. Cheerleaders who act in verbal support of the core, and spectators or observers. The latter create an arena for the action of the active core.

At Heysel Stadium the active core was the group of Liverpool fans who charged the Juventus supporters. These fans (all men) likely had strong feelings about the insults they were receiving from the Juventus section. Also, both press and television reports indicated that some of the Liverpool fans, because of poor ticket control, were directed into Section Z.

The Presence or Absence of Channels of Communication

When looking at channels of communication, the researcher using Smelser's model tries to discover whether or not there are normative ways present for expression of grievances. Surprisingly, considering the scope of soccer worldwide, there are few ways to express disagreements among fans. One way is the singing of short songs or chants between different sets of supporters. For example, it is common among English fans to sing the score to the other side. Thus Aston Villa followers might sing or chant, "1–nil, 1–nil" to Leeds fans, while waving the right index finger to illustrate their score of one in the air. Another way of expressing happiness or joy is by singing a victory song such as, "We are going to Wembley," when one's team scores. Wembley refers to the site of the most important match in England—the F.A. Cup championship.

These two methods are used to express winning. Another way that a soccer crowd can express itself is by whistling to protest stalling or a referee's poor decision, or by calling for the end of the match.

These methods for crowd expressions of joy or hostility are tied primarily to the events of the match, to actual play. Thus, Liverpool or Juventus fans had few if any normative ways of responding to insults before the match. Liverpool fans turned to nonnormative modes of response, including obscene shouts, and gestures, missile throwing, and lastly, fighting.

Communication among the Aggrieved

To understand the communication of the situation just before the hostile outburst happened, it is necessary to describe conditions on the terraces. First, most European football grounds do not have the amenities one sees in many American sports complexes. They are located, particularly in the first division, in large cities, often in run-down sections of the city.

More important than park location are the standing terraces which are very much part of the tradition of football.[4] Terraces do not have seats, rather they are concrete steps with barriers at waist height behind which fans, generally young fans, stand. Terraces are located behind the goals, but can be parallel to the field as well. The terraces are slanted, quite sharply in places, and go as high as three or four stories. In walking up and down, one has to be careful not to trip and fall.

Heysel Stadium in Brussels was built into 1930 (*Daily Express*, 5/31/85, p. 20). The terraces were in disrepair. The concrete was crumbled and chipped and the barriers rusted. I noticed weeds growing on the terraces, indicating the broken-up quality of the concrete. Supporters in both sections had to be careful as they moved around the terraces because of the uncertain footing. This was exacerbated by the angle of terraces, which is not as steep as in some stadiums, but still made movement difficult. This restriction in movement limited the extent that Liverpool fans could communicate with each other. Second, there would have been considerable noise on the terraces, with singing and chanting of songs in support of the two soccer teams. Lastly, the terraces were filling up but not packed. Thus, it would have been possible for some lateral movement on the terraces.

These three conditions limited communication among the aggrieved. My experiences on English terraces suggest that shared communication probably could not have reached more than 25 to 40 yards from the attack point on the fence. Having said this, it should be remembered that considering the increasingly dense conditions on the terraces at forty-five minutes before the match, 25 to 40 yards would have included a few thousand football supporters. In summary, all the conditions for structural conduciveness were met: sources for blame were identified; there were few channels for expressing grievances; and communication among the aggrieved was limited but possible for a critical mass of people.

Structural Strain

Smelser's model indicated that strain should be examined by the analyst at the levels of values and norms: Is the sports violence limited to strains located in larger community problems (value strain) or to the sport (normative strain)?

Let us look at the value question first. The most important value that would have been under attack at Heysel stadium would have been nationalism. In other words, were Liverpool fans responding to supporters of Juventus because of insults about Englishmen, England, the Queen, or Britain? In order to answer this question of nationalism, it is necessary to have criteria for nationalism. Gerald Newman (1987, pp. 54–58) proposes such criteria in his analysis of the rise of English nationalism. He argues that nationalism is (1) more than mere patriotism; indeed it is a sense of national freedom and solidarity, (2) all encompassing, including all of a nation's political, economic, and social affairs, (3) an ideology which serves to transform the emotional and intellectual bonds of a society, (4) based on the activities of artists and intellectuals who help develop nationalistic feelings, and (5) seen as a national crisis about the impact of external influences on society as well as domestic elites.

In examining the entire range of materials, nothing remotely fits these criteria of nationalism. For example, in looking at photographs, there is no evidence to indicate that banners, posters or anything else were generating anti-British feeling from the Juventus side. In addition, there were reports of some fraternizing among Juventus and Liverpool supporters in the morning and afternoon of match day. However, even though there is no clear evidence of nationalism, it is likely feelings of patriotism might be present. When football fans from two European countries come together, such feelings can lead to hostilities. In the Heysel riot there is, again, no clear evidence that this was the case. Thus, we must look elsewhere for feelings of strain.

Strain, then, seems to be more likely at the level of norms. What norms? Photographic evidence suggests that a strong possibility would be insults against the Liverpool team. Supporters of Liverpool, as one picture in *Sports Illustrated* clearly shows

(Gammon 1985, p. 23), flew the red and white with pride. Liverpool displays can be seen on scarves, flags, badges, hats, and caps. On the facing page, the same is true for Juventus black and white.

How might Liverpool have been insulted? First, through gestures and other insults in the manner described earlier, although Italian supporters may not have understood their significance. However, it is doubtful that Liverpool fans would have responded to these insults with a physical attack. Rather, they would have responded in kind with gestures, chants, and songs about the Juventus team.

The next level of strain would have come from the missile throwing, including chunks of concrete, bottles and flagstaffs. Again, the response, in my view, would not have been a physical attack, but rather the Liverpool fans would have thrown missiles or would have begun spitting on the Juventus supporters. Spitting is a common response to the insults from other teams' followers.

Most probably the major source of normative strain was the attack on a Liverpool fan who unhappily got on the "wrong" side of the fence. One account (*The Times*, 6/1/85, p. 4) suggests that a small group of Juventus supporters began fighting with a young Liverpool fan who was in Section Z. Liverpool fans in Section Y attempted to go to his aid and the melee began.

Thus, there seem to be violations of norms, verbal insults, missile throwing, and attacks on a fan that moved a small portion of Liverpool fans into action. In summary, the source of strain is difficult to pin down. This analysis favors normative strain position particularly in terms of insults to teams, but, it is possible that nationalistic or patriotic feelings were also factors in the outburst.

Growth of a Generalized Belief

Smelser argues that certain subdeterminant conditions encourage the development of hostile beliefs. These are labeled ambiguity, anxiety, assigning of responsibility, a desire to punish, and feelings of omnipotence. Each subdeterminant is sufficient to stimulate a shared belief. Thus, the analyst, using

Smelser's model, is required to identify evidence that supports the presence of at least one subdeterminant. The analysis begins with the assigning of blame as there seems to be no evidence to support the existence of feelings of ambiguity or anxiety.

Assigning of Blame

Liverpool supporters saw Juventus fans as the source of trouble, as opposed to police, vendors or even events on the playing field. The first two charges were directed at Juventus fans as well as the last and fatal attack.

The police, players and playing pitches have all received the ire of English soccer fans at one time or another. For example, English fans have been known to carry out a pitch invasion when their team was about to lose a match. At Heysel, none of this happened. The police were not attacked nor were players on the pitch. The opponents to blame, for Liverpool fans, were the Juventus supporters.

Desire to Punish; Feelings of Omnipotence

These variables are more analytically useful when combined because a desire to punish and feelings of omnipotence tend to work hand in hand. Liverpool fans near the fence wanted to harm Juventus supporters on the other side. Photographs show Liverpool supporters, as identified by colors, taking pipes from the fence and preparing to swing at the Juventus fans. Feelings of omnipotence are more difficult to document, but it seems reasonable to assume that the small group of Liverpool supporters who went at the Juventus fans felt that the police or Juventus fans would not respond to the attack. This is particularly true in view of the fact that there was no coordinated response to the initial charge of the Liverpool supporters.

In summary, the data indicate that three of the five subdeterminants which facilitate the growth of a generalized belief were likely present among members of the Liverpool fans at Heysel. That is, feelings of blame assignment, a desire to punish, and omnipotence influenced fans nearest the fence. The question is, how widely shared were those beliefs? How generalized were they? Given the physical structure of the terraces it is likely that the shared feeling was distributed among the active core, cheerleaders and spectators who were twenty-five to forty yards from the fence. Beyond this it would not have been possible for shared feelings of blame, punishing and omnipotence to develop. Indeed, on both sides, most beyond this range probably did not know a hostile outburst was underway.

Mobilization for Action

Mobilization for action refers to those subdeterminants that influence the shape of a hostile outburst. These include leadership, the organization of the outburst, and its phases.

Leadership

For Smelser, leadership can stem from persons or events. In reference to persons, there does not seem to be any strong evidence of leaders in the Heysel riot. It seems that about 20 or so Liverpool supporters actually carried out the final charge. But it would be too strong a statement to call them leaders. There were suggestions that extreme right-wing groups led the charge, but the Popplewell Report (1986, p. 7) concluded, "There is no evidence to suggest that any National Front members were involved in the riot. . . ."

Events structured the outburst. At Heysel, it is likely that when the fence gave way it stimulated the actions of the Liverpool supporters to carry out further attacks. Attacks on fences separating supporters occur often at big matches in England. My experience is that these fences in England are much more substantial than the one at Heysel. It is likely that the Liverpool supporters were quite surprised when they breached the fence.

Organization of the Hostile Outburst

Here Smelser's model directs the analyst to look at preexisting crowd structures, ecological factors, and social control. The first two variables are easily combined while the third is discussed in the next section.

The preexisting crowd structure refers to the degree of coordination among crowd members prior to the beginning of the hostile outburst. An English soccer crowd is fairly well organized before and during a match. This comes from physical symbols including the wearing of scarves, hats, favors and pins; coordinated gestures and other physical movements such as jumping up and down and moving side to side; and chants and songs. In addition, the vast majority of English fans had traveled in groups from Liverpool to the Heysel stadium. Most supporters felt themselves connected to other supporters on the terrace. In other words, in contrast, for example, to an American baseball World Series game, there was a consciousness of kind that could be called a pre-existing crowd structure.

The second dimension of the organization of the hostile outburst refers to ecological factors. The configuration of the terraces has been noted. In addition, a second ecological variable that is important is the easy access that the Liverpool fans and the Juventus supporters had to one another. Most major competitions in Europe use extensive segregation procedures to keep supporters separated. This did not happen at Heysel stadium. Indeed, it is likely that many fans on both sides were surprised by the limited segregation procedures. However, Belgium soccer authorities did not control ticket sales; thus tickets were supposed to be sold only to Belgians and other "neutrals" were in fact sold to Italians (Popplewell, 1986, pp. 71–72).

Initial and Derived Phase

The hostile outburst is divided into two basic phases that the Smelser model describes. Before looking at this it seems appropriate to describe the violent behavior of the supporters. It is assumed that this behavior is always preceded by shouts and gestures of obscenity. This typology (Lewis, 1982a) suggests the order in which the behavior happens:

- *Throwing Missiles:* Small groups of fans propelling bricks, beer, coins, pieces of metal or bottles at players, opposing fans, officials, or the police.

- *Vandalism:* Small groups of fans, in concert with each other, destroying property.
- *Fighting:* Small groups of fans throwing punches at players, opposing fans, officials, or the police.
- *Disrupting Play:* Small groups of fans running on the pitch, field, or court, and halting play.

The initial phase began when Liverpool supporters shouted obscenities and threw missiles at the Juventus supporters. This was followed by surges and fighting among small groups of Liverpool and Juventus fans. We do know something about the characteristics of the Liverpool fans from the legal proceedings.

In the Fall of 1987, twenty-five football supporters were extradited to Belgium and charged with manslaughter.[5] All were white males, with most from the Liverpool area. In the Spring of 1988, the Liverpool fans were released on bail and returned to England pending trial in the Fall. These data need to be evaluated carefully. We do not know if the indicted fans were the ones that led the charge that resulted in the crowd crush which caused the fatalities. However, it is likely that the characteristics of those indicted represent the characteristics of the fans who led the attack on the Juventus supporters.

The derived phase of the hostile outburst happened when Juventus supporters, in an effort to get away from the missile throwing and fighting, pushed and shoved against other Juventus fans. This resulted in pressure against the wall on the side of the terrace causing the deaths and injuries to the Juventus soccer fans. In other words, the tragedy was not caused directly by the fighting and missile throwing, but by the crush that was created when the Italian fans tried to avoid the hostile outburst.

In summary, all of the conditions proposed by the model of mobilization were present. There was leadership primarily from events. The organization of the hostile outburst was shaped by pre-existing crowd factors and ecological conditions. Lastly, the riot moved through an initial phase of hostile outburst to a derived phase of a crowd crush.

Social Control

For Smelser, social control is an important part of any collective behavior episode. It is not distinct and separate, but is part of the value-added process at any stage. At Heysel stadium there were several breakdowns in this social process. The most notable ones were, at first, the lack of discipline and self-control of the Liverpool fans, second, the failure of the Belgium officials to control ticket sales, and third, the improper use of Belgium police.

Liverpool Supporters

Without doubt the lack of restraint by a small number of Liverpool fans was the major cause of the riot. The hostile outburst began with obscenities, moved through vandalism, missile throwing and finally the charges resulting in the fatalities. At each point in this sequence the Liverpool supporters could have opted out of the process and, no doubt, some did. But why didn't reason and good sense prevail? It was noted earlier that English football fans have few legitimate mechanisms for expressing anger and hostility. When the small number of Liverpool supporters made the third rush that resulted in the deaths, they likely thought they were acting properly by attempting to take over a part of the Juventus end. While this behavior is clearly unacceptable in terms of general social norms, it is not unexpected behavior in the hooligan subculture. Of course, the results were tragic. Thus while one must deplore the lack of self-control, it is possible to understand it in the context of hooligan values.

Segregation Procedures

The separation of European soccer fans according to the team they support is called segregation. It is always used at major soccer matches. Indeed, at international matches it is the basic procedure for crowd control.

The separation of rival sets of football fans is achieved in several ways. First, fans are located in different places in the stadium, usually at opposite ends of the pitch. Fans cannot move around because physical barriers, usually stout fences, are placed at varying intervals throughout a stadium. Second, at very important matches, generally championships, human barriers are used to segregate fans. One way these buffer zones are achieved is by placing "neutral" fans between sets of rival supporters. For example, the host country's fans would be placed between the supporters of the two teams playing the match. Another way this buffer zone is achieved is to actually put a line of police in the terrace which serves to separate the fans. This is the procedure English police use at important matches (Lewis, 1982b).

At Heysel segregation failed. Segregation of supporters was to be controlled by ticket sales. This is where the procedure first broke down. The Belgian House of Representative's Commission noted (Popplewell, 1986, pp. 71–72):

> The ticket sales . . . got completely out of hand. It has been established that a large number of tickets for Section Z (a neutral zone where there should under no circumstances have been any Italian supporters) were sold to Italians . . . large quantities of tickets were sold to travel agents, football clubs and others without their having been asked to give any written guarantee whatever that they would not sell tickets to Italians. The sale of tickets at Heysel Stadium (theoretically restricted to five tickets per person) was organized in such a way that anyone, including Italians, could get tickets for Section Z without any problems at all. This is in contravention not only of UEFA directives but also the arrangements agreed before the match. Such a procedure was bound to create a black market.

Liverpool and Juventus fans were incorrectly placed next to each other. Juventus supporters were sold tickets in section Z that was supposed to be for "neutral" Belgian fans. In addition, Liverpool supporters were actually directed into sections where Juventus fans were located.

Second, the physical barriers separating sections Y and Z were clearly inadequate. Senior officers must have inspected the ground before the match and should have noted the poor quality of the fencing. However, it is likely that nothing could have been done to improve the physical strength of the fencing after such an inspection since making changes in the physical makeup of a soccer stadium requires considerable effort and time on the part of the police.

Police Procedures

This analysis of social control has noted the lack of self-control of Liverpool supporters as well as the failure of segregation procedures. However, some responsibility also falls on the police for not preventing the riot in the first place.

In Belgium there are two distinct police forces. There is Belgium police and the gendarmerie (rijkswacht), which is part of the army. In the stadium there was a distinct division of labor. The Belgium police were responsible for one-half of the stadium while the gendarmerie controlled the other half. The trouble which eventually led to the crowd crush was in the gendarmerie's half of the Heysel stadium.

The social control errors can be divided into two categories. First, there were not enough Belgium police and gendarmerie inside Heysel stadium before the match. Several sources estimate that there were about 1,000 police on duty, but most were outside Heysel on traffic control. When the rioting began there were a little over 100 Belgium police in the stadium and a small number of gendarmerie, although the exact number is unknown (K. Van Limbergen, 1988). Of course, the police and gendarmerie were spread all over the stadium, which is very large. For example, it was reported that supporters at the opposite end of the pitch from where the wall collapsed could not see what was going on.

The second category of errors began when the rioting started. The gendarmerie should have moved into the terrace when they observed the fence being breached. However, they did not because they had too few gendarmes near Sections Y and Z to go effectively into the crowd. In addition, because of the crowd density as well as the limited number of gates, access to the attack point would have been extremely difficult.

Why was the response of the gendarmerie so ineffective? The work of two Dutch sociologists (discussed elsewhere in this issue) provides us an answer to the question. Paul 't Hart and Bert Pijnenburg (1988) describe the organizational errors of the gendarmerie. First, as noted earlier, it was completely unexpected that Juventus and Liverpool supporters would be placed next to each other. Second, there were very few gendarmes in the X, Y and Z sections of the terraces. Third, the gendarmes did not know how to react to the fighting because of unclear guidelines. Fourth, they did not have a sound decision-making system because their senior officers were outside the stadium dealing with a minor incident when the rioting began. Fifth, calling for reinforcements was difficult because of the spectator noise and poor radio equipment.

In summary, riot was facilitated because social control broke down in three general areas. First, and most importantly, Liverpool supporters acted in a highly antisocial manner understandable only in the context of the soccer hooligan subculture. Second, Heysel authorities failed to carry out proper segregation procedures, particularly in reference to ticket sales. Third, gendarmerie were incorrectly placed before the riot and failed to respond properly when the riot began.

Conclusion

This essay has examined the Heysel stadium soccer riot using Smelser's model of collective behavior. The riot, one of the worst in the history of soccer fan violence, occurred in May 1985, before the European Cup final in Heysel stadium in Brussels, Belgium. This analysis, based on primary and secondary data, was able to locate evidence for the determinants and subdeterminants proposed by Smelser's model.

What principles can one derive from this case history? Two general points should be noted. When looking at the determinants of structural conduciveness and strain in the Heysel riot, it seems reasonable to conclude that these conditions are present at almost every major international soccer match, including World

Cup play. Thus, the possibility of a "Heysel" is always present when international championship soccer is played. If this is true, then the second point becomes even more important—the determinant of social control. At Heysel the breakdown in control was widespread. First, there was the appalling behavior of some of the Liverpool supporters. Second, the control of fan segregation by football authorities was inadequate by any standard. Third, the handling of the crowd by the gendarmerie was poor. But there is hope. All three social control failures can be eliminated in future matches. Fan behavior can be improved; ticket management can create satisfactory segregation of fans; and police can be trained in effective crowd control tactics.

The Heysel riot stimulated much discussion and debate in England and in Europe about the "English" disease of soccer hooliganism and what can be done about it. In a narrow sense this is appropriate. Yet, in a larger one, as the analysis of structural conduciveness and strain has shown, the problem is not strictly an English, Belgian or Italian one, but rather is one for all international soccer authorities to focus on. To die or to be seriously hurt as a result of a soccer riot is (like the plot of the lives of people in an Albert Camus novel) utterly absurd. Heysel challenges all of those interested in international soccer to work to prevent such a riot from ever happening again.

Notes

Date of acceptance for publication: 1 August 1988. Address for correspondence: Jerry M. Lewis, Department of Sociology, Kent State University, Kent, OH 44242

1. This is a revised version of papers presented at the 1985 NASSS meetings in Boston, Massachusetts and the University of Ulster, Jordanstown, Northern Ireland in 1987. I wish to thank Jeffrey H. Goldstein, Diane L. Lewis, Frank Romano and Kris Van Limbergen for their comments on this article.

2. A note on terminology is needed. "Heysel" is the French word for the stadium while "Heizel" is the Dutch word. In English writing the term "Heysel" is generally used and I have followed this convention.

3. I am indebted to Catholic University of Leuven students: Peter t'Hooft who provided me the papers and Danny Verhaeghe who did the translations.

4. In Belgium terraces are called tribunes.

5. The twenty-sixth supporter was in jail in England on other charges.

References

Gammon, C. 1985. "A Soccer Riot." *Sports Illustrated* June 10, 22–30, 35.

Lewis, J. M. 1972. "A Study of the Kent State Incident Using Smelser's Theory of Collective Behavior." *Sociological Inquiry* 42:87–92.

———. 1982a. "Fan Violence: An American Social Problem." In *Social Problems and Public Policy*, ed. M. Lewis, vol. 2, 175–206. Greenwich, CT.: JAI Press.

———. 1982b. "Crowd Control in English Soccer Matches." *Sociological Focus* 15:417–23.

Newman, G. 1987. *The Rise of English Nationalism*. New York: St. Martin's Press.

Popplewell, Mr. Justice O. 1985. *Committee of Inquiry into Crowd Safety and Control at Sports Grounds*. Final Report. London: Her Majesty's Stationery Office.

———. 1986. *Committee of Inquiry into Crowd Safety and Control at Sports Grounds*. Final Report. London: Her Majesty's Stationery Office.

Smelser, N. J. 1962. *Theory of Collective Behavior*. New York: The Free Press.

't Hart, P., and Pijnenburg, B. 1988. Het Heizeldrama: Rampzalig organiseren en kritieke beslissingen. Trans. M. Mercy. *Sporta* 42:120–32.

Van Limbergen, K. 1988. Personal interview, May 30. Leuven, Belgium.

Index

About the Author

Jerry M. Lewis, now a professor emeritus, has been a sociology professor at Kent State University since 1966. He obtained his bachelor's degree from Cornell College, his master's degree from Boston University, and his doctoral degree from the University of Illinois (Urbana).